BLAMING + START TALKING

Developing a Dialogue for Getting Public Education Back on Track

Deborah

TEACHER
TIM MULLEN, PHD

Thank You for all you do
To prepare Teachers of Science

Tim Mullen

UNITED WRITERS PRESS
ASHEVILLE, NC 28803

STOP Blaming & START Talking

ISBN-13: 978-1-945338-14-4

First edition 2016

Published by:

United Writers Press
Asheville, N.C. 28803
828-505-1037
www.UnitedWritersPress.com

For quantity discounts, please contact the author at:

tim@teachertimmullen.com

Dedication

To my peers in the most important profession in America. I am proud to be a teacher and hope that my telling this story will help teachers, the teaching profession, and public education in the United States;

To my wife Loretta, who tolerated my job change to a profession that paid a fraction of what I'd earned before and would herself leave the practice of law to become a teacher;

and to my three daughters—
who though young when my journey began, understood when I came home exhausted, took naps before supper, and graded papers while waiting for them at soccer practice.

Contents

Preface

This book is not research-based. It doesn't have footnotes or citations on every page—it is based on my perception, from the classroom, of what's happening, why, and how we can make things better. My primary goal in writing it is to share my thoughts with you and, knowing that my experiences and concerns are by no means the only ones affecting our public schools, to invite you to share your experiences and concerns with me. I believe that if we commit to listen to each other, consider the many components that affect public education both positively and negatively, and then combine our creativity, we can develop a workable and effective plan for changing policies that have tied teachers' hands for almost three decades and applying evidence-based solutions to the issues that educators confront every day.

I write this as an American citizen, a parent of three grown daughters with grandchildren in the future, a taxpayer concerned about my home's property values and the uses of my property taxes devoted to supporting local schools. But I write it mostly as a teacher in the classroom every day.

There are many "experts" criticizing public education and teachers, but few of the "experts" seem to be teachers, who are the only ones with the expertise and perspective required to identify and solve the problems we face. It's time the profession is returned to the position in our society it deserves. It's time we are allowed to get back to doing the jobs we were trained to do instead of teaching to standardized tests that are meaningless in any real way to the students required to take them or the world those students will one day inhabit. It's time that the people who have spent a few years or a lifetime in the classroom to lead the conversations about what to do going forward.

It's time to STOP blaming and START talking.

Join me.

Timothy M. Mullen, Ph.D.
June 30, 2016

Chapter 1
Introduction

Public education—and public school teachers in particular—have been on the receiving end of criticism and blame for quite some time for a host of ills, many of which are beyond their control. And yet, although there has been a plethora of "experts" proposing and selling their "fixes," the voice of the greatest experts—teachers—has been largely ignored. As I said in the preface, it's time for that to stop.

I am a teacher and I have a proposal. Let's stop the finger-pointing and look at public education for what it is—a complex system of components and influences that must be acknowledged and factored into any substantive plans for improvement. Education is an ecosystem in which, like all other ecosystems, there is a delicate balance. Everything influences or has outright impact on virtually everything else. Many components crucial to the successful education of our children and the influences that affect those components are seldom—if ever—acknowledged and discussed.

The whole topic of public education in America needs to be examined in a way that it has not been for a long time. For-profit companies participate in regular self-examinations—the process is called planning and logistics. In the military, it's called tactical and strategic planning. But education's policymakers—especially those who have never stood in front of a classroom—don't. Instead, they offer little more than band-aids consistent with indefensible political platforms and often contribute to making existing issues worse. Examining the entire ecosystem is the only way we can hope to realistically improve public education in America and get it back on track.

Having said that, I do not profess to have "the" cure for the "broken state of education" in the United States. In fact, that's the point. I'm not sure it's broken, and if it is, there is no single black and white cure.

This book is my attempt to look at the state of public education from within. The topics you'll read about here have been discussed in school lounges for years, but they've not been brought together in one place. In part, that's because most teachers stay quiet, close their classroom doors, and do the best they can to do what they hired on to do—teach children the knowledge and skills they need to thrive as adults. They don't want to "rock the boat" because they're afraid to say anything for fear of how it will be perceived and because they've seen their counterparts lose their jobs for reasons beyond comprehension.

And yet, I submit that we're the only ones who know what's going on in our schools and what it will really take to change the state of public education today. I am not a consultant, elected official, university professor/

researcher, businessperson, radio talk show host, talking head on cable TV, or reform package salesperson. I do not speak as a parent, although I raised three daughters who attended public schools. I speak as a public school teacher, an "insider."

It is not my goal, however, just to respond to the critics—those "outsiders" whose agendas are generally based on some special interest other than that of improving our schools. It is my goal to propose a way of thinking about public education that has long been lacking in the dialogue.

The discussion must be comprehensive, and the approach must take an organized and thoughtful process, led by those who are living inside of the system every day, one in which coherent planning, implementation, and evaluation of results is ongoing.

Teachers are by no means the absolute authorities. Families, communities, and a multitude of other influences must also be considered when talking about raising children to be the successful adults that will contribute to the growth and well-being of the future of America. But although we are only one facet of the system, we are perhaps the most obvious group to lead the discussion—facilitators who have the children for seven hours a day, 180 days per year. Like customer service professionals in other industries, we are the closest to the ground, the people in touch with the primary "customers," our children. At the end of all the controversy, discussions, blame, criticism, fault finding, bashing, and negativity—it is the students who are suffering in the short and long term, and, in the end, they are all that matters.

This book is organized to lead us all through the first steps toward developing a comprehensive and coherent strategic plan to make public education stronger in America. That means getting on the same page with respect to the long-term goals we have for education. It means examining whether or not the goals we think we want are reasonable, based in reality, and attainable in the time frames we suggest; defining how we will measure our progress toward the achievement of those goals; honestly assessing where we are relative to the goals, what has worked and what hasn't, and laying a course together. To that end, here is a summary of what is addressed in this book.

Chapter 2: The Current Discussion. What are the topics and positions that are being discussed by elected officials, parents, media, and others? Are those topics relevant or red herrings?

Chapter 3: What Do We Want? To improve public education, there must first be a consensus with respect to what schools should be doing. But a consensus between whom? Who are the stakeholders and whose opinions should carry the most weight? What do we expect the outcomes of education to be? Are those expectations based in reality? What obstacles must be addressed before we can begin the actual journey?

Chapter 4: Pressures Outside the Classroom. What social, cultural, societal ills and political agendas stand in the way of public education's ability to fulfill the objectives we have? Are the policies and mandates in place helping or hurting us?

Chapter 5: Pressures Inside the Schools. What are schools already doing to try and ameliorate the issues discussed in Chapter 4 so that teachers have a fighting chance to actually do the job they were hired to do?

Chapter 6: Pressures Inside the Classroom. How are increasing class sizes, rising numbers of children whose basic needs are not met, an over-focus on high-stakes test scores, and lagging parental involvement affecting the motivation of students and the time and quality of known instructional techniques?

Chapter 7: The Effects of Politics, Sports and the Media on Public and Parental Perceptions. How have the negative political discourse, overemphasis on sports, and sensationalistic media outlets impacted parental perceptions of public education and parental attitudes toward teachers and the process of education itself?

Chapter 8: The Students Themselves. What challenges and obstacles do students present?

Chapter 9: The Teachers. Teachers love teaching and the children they work with. How can they get back to doing the jobs they hired on to do?

Chapter 10: The Edu-System: A Holistic Approach for Looking at Public Education. Improving public education requires the acknowledgment by all stakeholders and players that, like a living ecosystem, public education is an institution in which multiple and interdependent factors play a role. What can we learn from studies that look at all of the factors affecting public education simultaneously that can demonstrate the folly of our recent policies and inform our future efforts?

Chapter 11: What's Next? An appeal from the author to direct stakeholders with ideas for how each sector can help or stop hurting public education.

Chapter 12: Conclusion. Once we decide what we want public education to do, i.e., its purpose, and consider the pressures from without and within, the challenges of both students and teachers, and reduce the influences of politics, professional sports, and the media, how do we proceed?

Chapter 2
The Current Discussion

Public education is frequently in the news, debated in legislative bodies, and tossed around in conversation. Are schools broken? Repeal the Common Core! What's with these test scores? Everything was fine before "No Child Left Behind" and "Race to the Top"! If schools were run like a business, we wouldn't be having these problems. Charter schools are the answer…

Let's take a look at each of these in turn.

"Public education is broken."

Is public education broken? No!

Do I think that schools could do better? Yes.

Do I think my church could do better? Yes. Do I think my family could do better communicating and keeping in touch? Yes. Do I think our politicians could do a better job legislating? Yes.

All organizations, people, and occupations are in processes of continuous improvement, but that doesn't mean they're broken. So, why don't we hear that other professions are broken? Lawyers don't win all their cases, doctors lose patients, and car mechanics don't get repairs right the first time every time. I asked for sweet potato fries with my burger last week and got regular fries, but I haven't heard that food service is broken.

So what is it that fascinates everyone with schools? I suppose one reason is that everyone went to school and has first-hand knowledge (good, bad, or indifferent) of what "school" means, so they consider themselves experts. (Never mind that their perspective is only from the student side of things.) Maybe it's because the topic of interest affects our children, which makes it far more personal. Maybe education is an easier target since teachers generally don't fight back like other professionals who come under attack.

When I turn off the noise and look at how schools perform now compared to "when I was a kid" (a common topic in parent-teacher conferences), schools are doing better than ever before and they're accomplishing far more.

For example, when I was a kid, in the 60s and 70s, there were few special education or gifted programs to meet the needs of those children who had above or below average abilities. Teachers taught to the middle—if you were "slow," did not like school, or had a disability, you dropped out and got a job at the mill. If you learned quickly and liked school, you went on to college if your parents could afford it or could arrange for a loan, or if you did so well you were eligible for a scholarship. If you immigrated to America and did not speak English, you were accepted, but the message was, "Learn English or fail."

Today, we have programs for gifted kids, children with physical handicaps and learning disabilities, and children for whom English is a second language. Sounds like an improvement to me.

The media, politicians, radio and cable news jocks, and whoever else wants others to listen, follow, or vote for them have been so vocal for so long now that the average citizen now believes that schools are broken.

Most teachers have had experiences with hostile parents who come to school conferences with their pre-conceived notions, but the vast majority of parents don't fall in that category. Numerous studies and surveys indicate that most parents are satisfied with their children's schools. They like the principal, their children's teachers, and the "climate" of their child's classrooms. "They must be talking about the other schools," they say, "because I like mine."

The negative perceptions have been created in people's minds by the talking voices/heads, not by personal experience. Look at test scores, for example. If comparisons are done properly, between similar groups and sample sizes, you will see that special needs children are doing better, children growing up in poverty are doing better, children from households that speak a language other than English are doing better, graduation rates are better than ever before, and so on.

The public, especially parents of school-aged children, need to see their own local numbers, not generalized national or state numbers. People need to see how the different sectors of our society perform in school, and *then* ask the hard questions about what isn't working.

I am not suggesting that there is no work to be done. Continuous improvement in education, as in any other "industry," is a must. But in general, public schools aren't broken. In fact, they're doing quite well.

"Standardized test scores are/aren't an adequate measure of student learning."

Who has the highest SAT average? Where does my state rank with the SAT, the NAEP (National Assessment of Educational Progress) nationally? Does that matter?

After a ranking is announced, the media, experts, and politicians feel a need to pontificate about what is wrong with public education instead of asking the purposes of the tests used, what the tests themselves actually measure, and if the scores actually correlate with ultimate success in college and the workplace. I'm convinced that those groups wouldn't be so quick to the fix if we weren't so fascinated with test scores.

Why have we become so enamored? I have a couple of theories.

An Obsession with Sports

Every day, scores are reported for every team, year round, so we've developed the habit of thinking numbers represent how successful we are. After all, no one wants their school to be second or third, let alone 12th nationally. Thanks to an obsession with sports, we have become a country of winners and losers.

That's all well and good as long as the comparisons are equitable and make sense. However, I have never seen scores for women's basketball compared with the boys' teams in high school. I have never seen Division III college teams compared with those in Division I. I have never seen high school Class A (fewer than 600 students in Georgia) compared to class AAAAAA (over 2,500 students), nor have I seen Special Olympic athletics compared to traditional Olympic athletics.

If North Dakota ranks number one in SAT scores, does it make sense to compare California's scores? How many students are there in North Dakota as compared to California? How many of those actually took the test? What rank were those students in their graduating class? Would they have been in the top 10% in a California school?

Some states only test the top 10% of their students, who are generally headed for college. Others test up to 80% of their future high school graduates. Does comparing those states make sense?

What is the demographic makeup of the test-takers? How did the African-American students in low socio-economic areas stack up against the whites in high socio-economic areas? What's the SAT comparison between the parents who graduated from Harvard vs. those who only completed high school, but have highly successful careers in skilled occupations?

Don't get me wrong—I like sports. I played them in high school, too. But an obsession with numbers and rankings, fueled by sports, is being unfairly applied to public education. We stop at the top 25 nationally ranked football teams and *never* ask who came in last.

Not so in public education. It's those schools who come in "last" that we focus on, as students and the SAT—and punish—compared as if all other things are equal.

Computers and the Ease of Number Crunching

Computers can crunch lots of numbers and crunch them fast, sometimes increasing our productivity. But, technology, for all of the advantages it provides us, has made it increasingly easy to oversimplify some things. It's the way we report and digest those statistical comparisons that counts.

We want to know who's best and who's worst, who's first and who's last, who made the most money, and who didn't. Give me a number!

The easiest way in education to generate those numbers is through the reporting of standardized test scores. They are easy to score and generate lots of statistics. Students all over the country take the Scholastic Aptitude Test or similar instruments. But the SAT also has shortfalls that are not often discussed. In fact, many colleges no longer require SATs for admission. So, if colleges are moving away from it, is it a good predictor of "success?" Not necessarily. But the scores *are* easy to use.

Oh, no! We've fallen behind Finland!

In 2012, the USA ranked 27th in math, 17th in reading, and 20th in science (standards of error notwithstanding) on the Programme for International Assessment (PISA). On the TIMMS (Trends in International Math and Science Study), conducted every four years, the average U.S. 4th grade math scores ranked 11th among the participating nations.

For the sake of discussion, let's talk about Finland, whose student test scores are higher on average than those in the U.S. Finland's students are considered to be some of the highest achieving in the world, and I am sure they are, but when I look more closely at the data, I see that in the case of Finland:

- The total population of the country is 5.4 million.
- Average test scores come from a smaller percentage of students, i.e., number of kids taking the tests vs. those not taking the test, is relatively small when compared to the USA.

- Finnish parents are generally well-educated and in socio-economic terms, most families upper middle class.
- Teachers have more freedom in decision-making, including curriculum and class environment, and are viewed as professionals.
- Teacher pay is comparable with that of other professionals—sending the message that they are viewed as equally important as engineers and businesspeople to the success of the country.

Japan and China also score higher on these tests when compared to the USA. No one seems to mention how education is the number one priority in those countries. Virtually from the time they are born, their students learn that education is key to being successful, and that they must do well in school. Parents and the community demand academic success.

Whereas this used to be largely true in the USA, many children now aspire to be sports stars and movie stars rather than academic stars, and many parents defer to their child's aspirations rather than reinforcing the importance of academic success. Children's heroes in the not too distant past were engineers and scientists—spin-offs from the space race, economic growth, and the drive to "win" the cold war. (More about that later.)

Although I often hear rhetoric about the "importance of education in the USA," as a teacher, it's not unusual for me to get an excuse for incomplete homework because *baseball practice interfered*. (I rather think it was the other way around. Don't you?) A math teacher in my school tells the story of talking to her class about our PISA rankings and the fact that Chinese students spend more time in school, have tutors, and are assigned lots of homework. A student raised her hand and asked, "When do they have time for sports?" (She was not joking.)

We do need ongoing educational reform. Diagnosing problems and designing solutions requires that we compare apples to apples, but we don't, because it isn't easy. In a world of instant gratification, people like numbers and rankings—and the simpler, the better. Statistics, whether meaningful or not, enhance political careers, increase viewership for media outlets, give states "bragging" rights.

But numbers alone will not help public education in America improve, because the issues, as noted before, are complex. Simplistic rankings only serve to spread negativity and divisiveness, and as the old adage says, ill winds blow no one any good.

"Governments should/shouldn't be involved in public education."

The U.S. Constitution begins with a preamble that explicitly states that one of the primary goals of the United States is to "promote the general welfare." It is easy for me to see public education as 1) a mechanism for promoting the welfare of all individuals and 2) an important part of supporting the free and informed "pursuit of happiness" described in the Declaration of Independence. To some degree, it makes sense to have a governing influence over that education that parallels the structure of government in general—some functions at the federal level, more autonomy at the state level, and the most at the local level.

Ultimate authority has fluctuated over the years, from local to state, from state to national, and back to state. Currently, the federal government doesn't have direct authority to tell state and local schools systems how to do things but it can and does tie criteria to requests for funding, and based on taxpayer demand for demonstrated impact for "our" money, seems reasonable on the surface. Right or wrong, officials of states and districts (who are tasked with managing school budgets) may not agree with federal mandates, but the strings of funding force them to comply.

The first Elementary and Secondary Education Act (ESEA) came as part of President Lyndon Johnson's "War on Poverty" legislation passed in 1965 to provide equal access of all citizens to quality public education. It was in 2001 (signed PL 107-110 January 8, 2002) that it was renamed the "No Child Left Behind Act." The ESEA of 2001 required that it be renewed in six years but it was not reauthorized until 2015, when it was renamed once again—the Every Student Succeeds Act (ESSA) of 2015.

Did we meet the goals established by the original ESEA? No. And, in my opinion, one of the main reasons was the application of free market principles, a misapplication courtesy of the "No Child Left Behind Act."

The new name implied that all children would be "successful" by the end of 2014, i.e., not "left behind." The unfortunate double standard and faulty logic of applying the rules of competition in public education, however, is clear. I can only imagine the reaction by any other profession if Congress passed legislation and called it by a similar title:

Doctors:	"No Patient Dies"
Dentists:	"No More Cavities"
Lawyers:	"No Party Loses"
Plumbers:	"No More Leaks"

Auto mechanics:	"No More Breakdowns"
Sales:	"No Sales Lost"
Corporate America	"No Company Too Big to Fail"
Wall Street	"No One Loses Money"

Not only are the rules of competition in the marketplace inappropriate, but just as no thinking person would expect all patients of a doctor to recover, the expectations schools are required to meet in order to gain funding are indefensible.

Where did it all start? In 1983, with a study called "A Nation at Risk," published by the Reagan Administration. Everything else that has transpired since, from the initiatives of Presidents George H.W. Bush and Bill Clinton to "No Child Left Behind," and President Obama's "Race to the Top" have been in knee-jerk reaction, and guaranteed to fail. (More later on the legacy of "No Child Left Behind.")

The question, I think, is not whether governments should be involved, but how? In 1979, President Jimmy Carter split the Department of Education from the former Department of Health, Education, and Welfare, creating the Department of Education and the Department of Health and Human Services, and elevated the position of Secretary of Education to a cabinet-level position. Its stated mission, according to the department itself, was/is:

> "...to promote student achievement and preparation for global competitiveness by **fostering** educational excellence and ensuring equal access..."

To use another business term, the "scope creep" is obvious, I think. Perhaps it is time to revisit the mission.

"Schools should / shouldn't be run like businesses."

In continuation of the mindset initiated by "A Nation at Risk" and codified by "No Child Left Behind," many say that we should "run schools like a business."

In the introduction to this book, I suggested that in general, our approach to education reform should be modeled after longstanding strategic planning practices utilized in the business world. But the analogy stops there. Although there are clearly some parts of school administration—like budgeting and financial planning and employer/employee issues, for instance—when individual schools are considered, the challenges are fundamentally different.

Where most businesses are private profit-driven entities, schools and school districts are public organizations. Businesses add value to something so you can sell it for more than you paid for it originally. You take raw materials and produce finished goods to sell.

If schools were to be run like businesses, we would take the raw materials (children) and add value to them so they could be sold for more than they would have been deemed to be worth when they entered school.

But businesses are selective about what raw materials they choose to then produce a product. If the quality of the raw materials are not up to a certain standard, manufacturers go to another source.

Public schools, on the other hand, must take in every child. They cannot be selective, nor should they be. The entire premise of public education as it was designed is to provide education to *every* child, irrespective of any other criterion.

If the rules of engagement in business are applied in the public education environment, there is an inherent conflict between doing what must be done to assure that every child succeeds...and the bottom line. To reach the same levels, it is simply a fact that some kids require more time (money) than others. The "quality control" of the business world requires that products that don't meet the standards are tossed out, recycled, practices in direct opposition to the mission of public education. Schools, by default, do the best we can to make every "product" the best it can be, all without the extra compensation profit-driven company employees expect for their efforts. If schools were businesses, if teachers failed at the falsely applied "business" mission, their salaries would be docked and they would be fired. As a public school teacher, I am a civil servant, and by definition, do not perform a for-profit function. I intrinsically agreed to the terms that, as a public employee, I would do what I needed to do to fulfill my responsibilities without the fear of penalty for failure to meet profit-driven goals.

When I worked in sales and developed proposals in response to RFPs, our standard process was to bid "cost plus" methods that paid us standard rates for work, but there were usually additional provisions built in for additional compensation in the event of unforeseen obstacles that might arise during the execution of a service contract. Think about the price of gasoline, for instance, something that isn't under the control of a manufacturer or customer, but affects the ultimate price of goods because it affects the costs associated with transporting those goods from the plant to the store. Unanticipated costs reduce profit margins.

The application of for-profit strategies to public schools creates an instant problem. Public schools enter into fixed fee contracts with charter management organizations (CMOs), involving specified amounts to be spent "per child." These contracts do not allow for amendments when some of the children take longer to learn than was originally predicted and could not have been anticipated (and by default, cost more to bring to standard). In a private business, extra costs erode the company's bottom line, and at some point, the company would default on the contract, be forced not to bid in the next contract cycle, or go out of business altogether.

This is not an option for public schools. There can be no default, no going out of business. No extras are built in to accommodate the higher costs. To continue the analogy from above, some kids have a longer road to travel to get where teachers are required to ensure they arrive, and require more money for gasoline, but no allowance for such exists in the structure of public school funding today…or in the minds of the general public.

Today's political environment makes the problem even worse, however. Over the past several years, some state legislatures are not only not funding with an eye toward contingency planning, but are reducing the amount of money allotted overall, requiring schools to maintain ever increasing performance standards with fewer and fewer teachers, larger and larger classrooms, and as will be shown, an increasing diversity among the students in everything from socio-economic status to language to race and ethnic origin.

"Charter schools and vouchers are / aren't the answer."

Many people confuse the term "charter" schools with "private" schools, ignorant of the fact that charter schools are still *public* schools, usually existing within established public school districts. Private schools are businesses that are privately financed, funded by tuitions and contributions, and by default, free of the rules governing public institutions, which are funded through the public sector, or governments.

The reason charter schools have become so popular are multi-fold:

1. Some parents want their children around "similar" children.
2. Elected officials do not trust public school teachers with the freedom they allow charter schools
3. Parents have been hearing for so long that public schools are broken that they have bought into the subterfuge and want an alternative.
4. Elected officials want to be re-elected, so they offer populist "choices" to their constituents in order to appease them.
5. The misapplication of business principles evoke visions of profits. Venture capitalists have invested billions in charter management organizations, and charter management organizations have contributed millions to advertise when referenda regarding charter schools appear on ballots and in support of re-election campaigns of public officials.
6. Large, philanthropic foundations offer funds to charter school initiatives, having also bought into the idea that the business models that made them successful are appropriate for education without evidence to support the contention.

Academies, parochial, and other private schools offer an alternative to public schools for parents with particular religious and/or philosophical reasons. Enrollment of children in private schools has stayed pretty much at the same for the last 50+ years—about 10% of all students. There is a niche served by private schools that I understand and can agree with.

The basic premise with charter schools is that they can be run without the overwhelming burden of legislation and mandates associated with regular public schools in the state or district in which they were granted their "charters." Granted, the idea that a school can be freed from many often superfluous restraints is appealing, and to some degree, we may only be able to differentiate between which restraints are superfluous and which aren't through the establishment of charter schools. But the unanticipated negative impacts of charter schools as they are presented today, if unchecked, may outweigh any benefits gained.

For instance, the whole idea of charter schools today sends an underlying and subversive message to teachers in regular public schools, which harkens back to the idea that public schools are broken. "You've been doing it wrong. We don't trust you." Many parents and the media have picked up on this message, which further adds to the distrust, whether justified or not, that many seem today to have for public education and teachers. Too many teachers hear this message and their spirits are dampened. Add to this message all the "reforms" thrown at us from the outside and the message only gets louder and more overwhelming. I have felt the impact personally.

Despite the fact that most general charter schools (defined as those schools not created for specific purposes, e.g., STEM or performing arts) are prohibited from criterion-based student selection, and lotteries are most often used to determine which students will be accepted, *charter schools have no control over who applies and who doesn't.* In one sense that is as it should be, but though it may be largely unconscious—overtly aimed at other issues of safety, comfort, and teacher-student ratios—a parent-driven racial, ethnic, cultural, and certainly economic segregation is silently occurring.

This is just a sampling of the ongoing conversations about public education, but they show the misinformation that's rampant and the complexity of the issues we face. And they also reveal that different people want different things.

Before we can move together toward solutions, we have to agree on one basic thing—what we want the outcomes to be.

CHAPTER 3
WHAT DO WE WANT?
WHAT ARE THE GOALS OF PUBLIC EDUCATION?

Before we can try to answer the question "What are the goals of public education?" we have to determine who will have the ultimate say in determining the answer. Who are the stakeholders? Whose opinions should hold the greatest weight? There are, by default, multiple goals, and depending on the goal and the number of people who will be impacted by success or failure to achieve the goal, some answers and opinions may weigh more heavily than others. Ultimately, everyone's input is needed, but it's especially important that groups with less realistic personal stakes in the state of education don't drown out those with more.

Who are the stakeholders?

There are both *direct* stakeholders and *indirect* stakeholders, but every citizen in our country must be included in one category or another. Let's examine some of the groups included in each subsection.

Direct Stakeholders

- **The children themselves.** It is their future we are talking about.
- **Parents.** It's their children we're talking about.
- **Professional Educators:**
    - **Teachers.** Because they interact with students every day, teachers are most prepared to begin the discussion.
    - **Public education leadership.** Superintendents, district leaders, professional organizations, and Boards of Education who provide the leadership, allocate funding, and oversee the systems within which teachers carry out their basic mission. Their involvement will inform how they direct their organizations to implement what ultimately is decided.
    - **Universities and colleges.** Institutions involved in the education of educators that advance research about how children learn, how to effectively deliver information and skills, and how to improve outcomes.
    - **Educational associations, non-profits, unions.** Curriculum-based organizations like the National Science Teachers Association (NSTA), National Council of Teachers of Mathematics (NCTM), National Council for the Social Studies (NCSS) and the National Council of Teachers of English (NCTE) and other organizations devoted to the teaching of specific academic subjects focus on subject-specific methods and concepts. Professional organizations like the National Education Association, American Federation

of Teachers on the national level, or in my state, the Georgia Association of Educators (affiliated with the National Education Association Union) and Professional Association of Georgia Educators, provide support and, in some states, collective bargaining with respect to education funding and the protection of teachers' rights and compensation. These groups are the professionals that are educated and trained in all aspects of education. They represent the many subject areas, teachers, methods, and interests. They are the professionals that are trained to deliver material to children to learn what has been identified important. This group of experts help those setting standards for schools, deliver the standards to children, and develop methods to evaluate progress toward learning what has been determined important. They need to be involved in defining success because they understand how children learn, develop, and mature. Their role in determining what 'success' is important because they are the ones responsible for delivering the required outcomes.

Indirect Stakeholders

- **Business leaders.** As we discussed in Chapter 2, one of the primary goals for education is to prepare students for success in the workplace and to be an integral part of our nation's leadership in the global economy.

- **Officials on the local, state, and federal levels.** From the bottom to the top in our national hierarchy, from local commissioners, mayors, and/or elders to governors and state and federal legislators, elected officials are tasked with collecting information from stakeholders and developing and guiding policies that facilitate implementation of effective programs.
- **The rest of us.** Which citizens should have a say about what happens in schools? Parents? If so, which parents? Religious groups? In a country where no religion gets special status under the Constitution, how would that work? The economies of different geographic regions depend on different things. To what extent, and at what level, should economic development leaders have a say?

Who should be involved in the dialogue

Our society is made up of a diverse and heterogeneous grouping of people with a multitude of needs, beliefs, and self-interests. While all of their concerns must be acknowledged and addressed, we must ask and answer the questions posed above, and determine a hierarchy for whose "say" holds the greatest weight. Countries that do not have such a large population and huge diversity of citizens have defined their goals for education more clearly. Teachers have clearly defined common goals and they deliver. Agreement is easier to achieve with a homogeneous grouping of citizens whose needs, beliefs, and self-interests are similar.

Sometimes it seems there will never be consensus. However, for the good of our children, and ultimately our country, there must be. The atmosphere of disagreement, ideology, and "my way" needs to be set aside to develop solutions. Everyone has a vested interest in the future of public education, whether we know it or not. So, from all of our stakeholders, what are some of the perceived goals of public education?

What We Say We Want

1) Prepare students for the workplace.

Business leaders say they want workers they can hire prepared to do the work. BUT there is no definition for what that preparation entails. Should schools prepare students for the skilled or unskilled labor market? (See #2) "Canned" high school and college degree programs cannot possibly prepare every student for every job. Business leaders need to be involved and provide more specific requirements for jobs that do not require college and those that do require college.

2) Create graduates with basic communication skills and strong work ethics.

I have many corporate friends and have read many articles interviewing executives about what they want in their workers. One common thread I've seen is that most employers want people who can communicate and have a good work ethic. A CEO once told me, "Give me people with good communication skills (written and oral) and with a good work ethic. I will teach them everything else they need to do the job for me." When I asked about what types of science, math, social studies topics he would like the graduate to have, he said it did not matter. Graduating alone showed him that they could finish something big and from there, he could teach him/her the specifics of the job.

That interaction was powerful for me. There is much discussion, debate, and hostility, at times, over the specifics of what should be taught, but most company executives just want people who can communicate and people on whom they can depend to show up for work and take care of the responsibilities they sign on for.

3) Educate all students to master a standardized curriculum for all subjects.

This has become most prevalent in the last 10-15 years and has primarily come from the federal (NCLB) and state legislatures. Because of that, teachers have moved toward investing their teaching energies on standards more than on the needs of individual students because standards are defined, detailed, mandated by their superiors, and appear easy to measure. Teachers are required to weave in some semblance of the other "purposes," but with "truth in grading" requirements and accountability, a limited amount of time, and the threat of their own livelihoods on the line, we naturally focus on the goal to prepare kids for the tests.

The result of this narrowing of focus is that the definition of success in public education has shifted from one focused on the unique needs, desires, and aptitudes of the individual student to one that attempts to lump all students together, assessing their progress according to a single criterion like "will pass standardized tests at year's end," which all-too-often ends in success for no one at all.

When high schools were created in the late 1800s, Harvard University played a major role in their creation. What was the goal? To prepare youth for college, hence the term "prep school." If a child wasn't going to college, eighth grade was generally the highest level students attended.

Because of this narrow focus, especially for those who graduated from college themselves, high schools are often considered to be no more than prep schools. Many states and/or school districts have all but eliminated what were highly successful "technical" tracks for their students who aren't "college material." But several studies published by various state departments of education have that found that fewer than 50% of the jobs available in their states required a college education. A decade ago, one state reported that only 20% of the jobs there required a college diploma. Yet another study found that, nationwide, only 30% of students who start college actually graduate with a degree. Is this another sign that we are pushing college onto children who need alternative education routes? For those who aspire to attend college, there is more to learn. But what is to happen to those kids who don't aspire to attend college?

I understand some of the hesitation with offering a trade school or non-college prep track to parents for their child. Because of the focus on college, it is implied that those who aren't "college material" are somehow less intelligent and their contributions to society less valuable. (To dispel that myth, consider just how important the plumber is when you're standing in sewage in your basement. Do you have the tools and "know how" you need?)

In this environment, how does a teacher approach a parent and say, "I don't think your child is college material? Maybe you should consider trade school." Most parents still want to see their child be more successful than themselves in their lives and we have created the perception that college is the end-all path to that success.

There used to be more dialogue about "skilled" and "unskilled" labor, instead of differentiating students on the basis of interest and aptitude. "Skilled" workers learned honorable trades often requiring hands-on talent, like plumbing, mechanics, or construction. A good friend of mine was 16 and, still in the eighth grade, dropped out. College wasn't an option for him, so he enrolled in a trade school—and has made a good living for his family as a welder.

In those days, administrators held kids back, and, if they didn't do everything necessary to pass, they were failed. "Everything necessary" meant doing all the assigned classwork, and passing the local exams (tests given by the teacher in the classroom to assess mastery of the material), without deadline extensions, re-takes, and extra help.

As passing standardized tests became the more urgent goal, because schools and teachers began to be evaluated based on the results of those tests, holding students responsible for fulfilling their part of the education compact (learning disabilities and other challenges not under their control excepted) was increasingly abandoned in favor of retests and providing extra chances to complete assignments with no penalty.

I don't think learning that you'll be given unlimited chances to do a job right is part of that standard curriculum we had in mind.

4) Create an educated populace to assure democracy is sustained.

Our nation's forefathers saw the necessity of creating and maintaining an educated population to keep the powers of democracy in check. With an uneducated population, dishonest leaders can become too powerful and greedy. When dictators or extremists take over a country, among the first things they do is attempt to dismantle the education system, because an uneducated populace is less likely to question a dictator's authority.

5) Ensure every American child is successful.

Here are but a few of the definitions of "success" that I've heard through the years. *I will know my child is successful if s/he:*

- Graduates from high school.
- Graduates from college.
- Gets a good job and raises a family.
- Makes lots of money.
- Becomes well respected in the community.
- Gets high test scores when compared to other children in his/her school.
- Gets high test scores when compared to other children in other states and countries.

Whose responsibility is it ultimately to define "success"? To what extent does public education realistically have a role in fulfilling all our expectations? Are those expectations reality-based? Do they take into account the needs of anyone other than "me"? Are there equally valid definitions of success that we've not considered?

When forming a strategic plan, before moving on to the next phase, the "wish list" of proposed goals must be evaluated systematically. One of the most popular ways taught in business circles over the past 30 years is the S.M.A.R.T. approach, attributed to an article written in 1981 in the journal *Management Review.* The words associated with each part of the acronym have been changed by some over time, but the concept remains the same. Is the goal Specific? Measureable? Attainable? Realistic? Time-Based?

Rather than what seems to be our regular process, to decide on an outcome without regard for whether it meets all of the criteria, what if we looked at each goal in turn? What does preparing students for the workplace mean? How does an educated populace relate to principles of democracy? What definition of success will we collectively determine to work toward? What are "basic communication skills"? Do we agree on what constitutes a good work ethic?

How will we measure progress with respect to each goal? Given the resources we have, an obviously important consideration, is it possible for us to achieve what we seek to achieve? Can we clearly demonstrate a connection between the programs we advocate for and the outcomes we demand? Have we set benchmarks for when and how we will achieve the goals?

If we don't have a clear idea of what we mean, if we refuse to even come to the table and seek a consensus about who will decide and who will be held accountable for achieving the goals, how can we move forward? If we fail to ensure that teachers have the authority to do what they know must be done, how can we ever expect to achieve anything at all?

We cannot.

What, for instance, is it—on a classroom by classroom, ground-level basis—that we expect teachers to accomplish? One thing is obvious, and as it always has been—to make available to children and youth knowledge about a variety of subjects and the greatest possible opportunities to learn and develop skills they will need in order to become as self-sufficient and successful as possible in their daily lives and in the workplace they will encounter tomorrow. That's hard to do when we have no consensus on what knowledge and skills they need.

What is too often lost in the rhetoric, however, is that teaching is *not just about facts and skills.* Competency in a subject area like math or life sciences isn't the only requirement. In fact, though its importance is obvious, and despite the fact of the information explosion, subject area knowledge, although necessary, may well be the least important requirement for successful teaching.

Instead, the first order of business for any teacher is, within the realm of his or her control, to *create an environment conducive to learning.* In other words, to do everything he or she can possibly do to ensure that every child has the greatest opportunity to learn whatever the subject matter, acquire and practice the skills we agree best allow them to learn, retain, and apply that subject matter, and then *continue the cycle of learning themselves.*

What *is* an environment conducive for learning?

What are the characteristics of an environment conducive for learning? On a very basic level, it's one that allows the greatest opportunity for children's brains to grow and change. Learning takes place when new neurons are formed and new connections are made between neurons that, in and of themselves, aren't necessarily connected. An environment conducive to learning is one that makes it easiest for those brain changes to take place.

When we learn that the object we sit in is called a chair, a neuron is formed. When we learn how to balance and take a step without falling down, a neuron is formed. When we hear and recognize the sound of our mother's voices, neurons associated with hearing and neurons associated with feelings of warmth and comfort are connected.

What happens that causes new neurons to form or existing neurons to wire together? Repetition, i.e., practice. In order for repetition to result in the necessary brain changes, we have to be focused and paying attention.

What do we pay attention to? Things that motivate us. What things motivate us? In simplistic terms, things that either 1) result in our feeling good or 2) help us avoid feeling bad.

Changes

In the days of one-room schoolhouses, teachers were tasked with teaching students of all ages in the same place at the same time, and, for the most part, they did it successfully, but not perfectly. Most of the time, those teachers were expected to be unmarried, without families themselves and other commitments. Communities were much more homogeneous—if you were a farmer's child, chances were good that every other child in your class was, too. The volume of knowledge students need to know now cannot even be sensibly compared to what students needed to know then.

No matter how hard some of us may wish for it, we cannot go back to an earlier time, nor do we really want to. No teacher should have to forgo having a family. Separate but equal, even if it were possible, doesn't work when the transitional nature of communities and workplaces demand that we have the skill to compromise, co-operate and co-exist in an increasingly complex world. In short, we must embrace change.

Having said that, however, even when we intellectually understand that change is necessary, we resist it.

Why is change so hard?

Everyone seems to want schools to change. "Improve" is usually the word used when the topic comes up, but either way, it is implied they are not working properly now. As you know by now, I disagree with that statement. In general, schools ARE working properly, but they do not exist in a vacuum. The impact of increasingly negative social and cultural issues is daunting. And the public and private discourse about improving education must focus on changing those social and cultural impacts that teachers and schools were never and should never be tasked with dealing with alone.

But no matter the semantics, why is change so hard? Several forces are at work that impact change in public schools. No one alone can be blamed, though some blame the teachers and unions. I don't agree. I recently saw that only 17 states allow teacher unionization of public servants and/or teachers. That leaves 33 that do not have unions to blame. Even in those states *with* unions, teachers don't resist change *that will improve the learning and eventual good of the children they work with.* They resist changes and demands that are counterintuitive with respect to that process.

Teachers want what is best for their students. Sure, we all know a few teachers whose only focus is themselves but their numbers are very small, and occur in no greater percentages than in any other group. Selfish people are everywhere. I know people at church who want what is best for themselves, not the church. I see friends in industry who want what is best for them and not their companies. To blame a few teachers for not wanting change and pretending that they are the reason schools are failing is not only farfetched, but an abdication of responsibility by people other than those who stand in front of a class of students every day.

Change takes time. Before becoming a teacher, I worked for the U.S. Army Corps of Engineers at a construction research lab. While talking to a research civil engineer one day, we talked about why change took so long in the field. He said that when his department's researchers came up with a better way to build something, it took an average of 17 years before it became common practice.

That was back in the 1980s, long before the internet and lightning-fast communication, but change in construction methods still doesn't happen overnight. Why thinking people would expect it of schools and teachers, even if the change is well-justified, is mind-boggling to me.

In education, a reason I hear often from my colleagues about changing is that whatever the change, "it won't last." There have been so many "reforms" pushed on teachers for so many years, with results expected in "a year or two," that none of them really believe they will ever be given the time they know it will take for them to fully understand and implement new programs.

I understand that we want results and we want them quickly. But I also understand that the source of so many "failed" policies and procedures in both the corporate and public spheres today is not a failure of policy. It's our failure to fully examine the positive and negative ramifications of our actions before they are undertaken, based on information provided by experts representing all of the direct shareholders. The legislators and media do not want to wait for the process of change to occur—of late, they are more interested in political expedience and ratings.

But, whether we think it should be or not, it is *not* human nature to change overnight. We are creatures of habit. Putting even changes we *want* to make for ourselves, such as lifestyle changes, weight loss, or watching less TV, take a while. To expect a large organization of diverse people to change within a year or two, completely revamping the ways in which they deliver information and are evaluated, and to expect the children themselves to respond to those changes as quickly, is neither realistic nor does it demonstrate even a basic understanding of people.

When the expected changes that politicians or central offices impose on schools and teachers do not occur as quickly as desired or "promised" to their constituents rather than reexamining the original time frames for their basis in reality, the now standard response seems to be to mandate and push down *more* new programs. As a result, many teachers and administrators have become jaded. They don't believe they will be offered the time to absorb, retrain, and truly integrate new curricula or programs into their methodologies (and the evidence suggests that they are right), so they carry on the best they can, adapting where they can, until the next policy or program comes along. In the end, what is measured and reported is the failure of the schools or the teachers—but not the lack of wisdom, maturity, and expertise of those doing the imposing.

The recurring theme of reform efforts also speaks to another underlying issue that impedes change—resistance from parents. I hear parents complain about schools, but when speaking to me, they are usually referring to other schools—not the one their child attends, parroting what they've heard from the media and politicians whose agendas have nothing to do with what's best for education or the reality of the options.

When I did the research for my dissertation, which focused on the effects of high-stakes testing on interdisciplinary teaching, I found that upwards of 80% of parents were satisfied with their child's teachers and school. But when questioned further, they believed that *other* public schools had issues and needed to improve. The "broken" schools must be "the inner city schools," a view which circles back to underscore other often skewed ideas also promoted by politicians and the media.

The bottom line is that individual organizational characteristics, industries, policies, and behavior all must be considered when change, even if it improves things, is orchestrated. By nature, smaller organizations can change faster than larger because there are fewer people involved with and impacted by the changes. Corporate organizations may be able to change faster than government bureaucracies because the rules and procedures are different and the "shareholders" are limited, whereas in government, every citizen within the jurisdiction has a say with his or her vote.

Add the extra scrutiny of the public when you are talking about change that impacts their children's lives (as opposed to raising a gas tax, for instance) and the process takes even longer. The sheer numbers of people required to make even simple changes come about—from districts to principals to teachers to students to parents and members of the general public whose children are either already adults or not yet born...you get the picture.

Like it or not, the public education system is made of humans. It takes humans time to change and if we take the process seriously, it should.

Give us clear direction, goals, and timelines that are well-documented and justified in bringing about the purposes we have agreed on, set a reasonable deadline for when the first measurements of progress will be conducted, convince us of the relevance to the outcomes you seek, and then leave us alone. We are professionals, and we will deliver. We do not need micromanagement, especially not by those who have never stood in our shoes and cannot possibly understand the challenges we face daily.

Tell us what you want and we will teach the children. We are trained professionals. Believe in our craft and the children, and we will do what is in our power to help children grow into the self-sufficient, well-informed, successful humans we all want them to be.

With all of the things that have changed, some haven't, however—how we learn, what makes learning more likely to occur, and what can interfere with the process. Those trained today for the occupation of teacher still learn Bloom's Taxonomy. The basics of Piaget's stages of cognitive development are the same as they ever were.

But for me, it's another theory, Abraham Maslow's hierarchy of needs, that most clearly frames the problems of public education today.

MASLOW'S HIERARCHY OF NEEDS

1. **Biological and Physiological needs** - air, food, drink, shelter, warmth, sleep
2. **Safety needs** - protection from elements, security, order, law, limits, stability
3. **Social needs** - Belongingness and Love, work group, family, affection, relationships
4. **Esteem needs** - self-esteem, achievement, mastery, independence, status, dominance, prestige, managerial responsibility
5. **Cognitive needs** - knowledge, **EDUCATION**, conceptual understanding
6. **Self-Actualization needs** - realizing personal potential, self-fulfillment, seeking personal growth and peak experiences
7. **Transcendence needs** - helping others to achieve self actualization

What are some of the obstacles to learning?

In short, an obstacle to learning is anything that interferes with any step in the process. To review, those include:

- Physical issues that distract from attention, like insufficient sleep, hunger, poor nutrition, lack of exercise;
- Safety issues that stimulate increased anxiety and fear, like bullying, school shootings, over-stimulation, drug use, deaths of classmates
- Emotional issues that sideline motivation, like family dysfunction, parental death and divorce, anxiety and depression
- Neurological issues that interfere with the "normal" neuronal connections, like dyslexia, dysgraphia, dyscalculia, attention deficit disorder

Notice that formal education is at Level 5 on the Maslow pyramid, and that all of the obstacles noted above relate to challenges occurring at Levels 1 through 4. According to Maslow's theory, in an optimal environment, needs must be fulfilled *in order.* Just as we can't learn to read until we have learned the alphabet, it is only when the biological, safety, social, and esteem needs of a child at levels 1, 2, 3, and 4 are satisfied that he or she can fully advance to the cognitive needs of Level 5—the only needs public education has always been designed to assist our children in fulfilling.

How many of the obstacles listed above are under a given teacher, principal, or superintendent's control? Truthfully, none. Is it reasonable to expect our schools to be able to deal with the explosion of new information and skills *and* somehow overcome the onslaught of social, emotional, economic, and neurological challenges that make the creation of environments conducive to learning exponentially harder today? Is that goal realistic? Attainable?

No. Teachers can only do so much by themselves. We need a new paradigm, one in which all stakeholders become aware of and acknowledge inherent challenges teachers face on a daily basis in providing environments conducive to learning. If we fail to support, undergird, and respect teachers, we will send the only professionals who have what it takes to achieve the outcomes we demand of public education running for the doors.

And then where will we be?

Chapter 4
Pressures Outside the Classroom

Both the rise of the middle class and the Civil Rights Movement occurred in the 1950s and 60s. As a result of the U.S. Supreme Court decision in *Brown vs. the Board of Education*, the first law was passed that detailed the role of the federal government in education. Its overarching intent was to provide a more equitable access to education for all Americans.

Many seem to believe that the issues that gave rise to these changes are no longer issues—that the problems those acts sought to address don't exist anymore. But despite these beliefs, in the educational sphere, racism, classism, and prejudice against other faith traditions, both overt and covert, still exist.

Meanwhile, the definition of the "middle class," as many had come to view it, has changed over the past 30 years, and fewer and fewer families fit that definition. Many who had reached a standard of living and expectations associated with the middle class are still recovering—and may never fully recover—from the effects of the recent Great Recession.

Increasing episodes of child abuse, human trafficking, and bullying are all symptoms of the economic stressors that affect us all. And the impact of these social changes on public education is enormous.

The longer I teach, the more convinced I become that the children who disrupt my classes, steal other kids' snacks, seek attention in negative ways, don't finish or turn in homework, or genuinely react with surprise when receive failing grades are proving Maslow's theory right in front of my eyes. As more children come to school hungry, homeless, in foster care, sleep deprived, etc., all of their natural energy for growth is co-opted in service of fulfilling needs that must be fulfilled before they ever set foot in my room.

Biological and Physiological Needs

Poverty and the Income Gap

The suggestion that income level affects achievement has been borne out for generations. What is it that makes that so? I don't think it's the dollars themselves that count. It's more likely the range of experiences money can provide, which in turn influence the possibilities we see for ourselves. Less money, fewer experiences. Over time, the children who aren't exposed to the same range of possibilities and opportunities have children themselves, and can't teach or model what they don't know themselves.

We humans are, by nature, imitators—we do what we see. As a rule, we emulate our parents — if they went to college, we expect to go to college and set our sights on what it took to get there, often applying to the same colleges and universities, majoring in the same subjects, following in their footsteps with respect to occupations and financial expectations. If our parents graduate from high school and go straight into the workplace, more often than not, so will we. If our parents drop out of high school, the odds that we will too are high. Our expectations define both our definitions of success and our individual realities—including the life experiences we seek and the level of achievement and mastery we aspire to.

But, it's one thing if a family has enough money to survive—a consistent and safe place to live, decent clothes, enough to eat—and quite another if not. As you will see in the next chapter about what's happening in schools today, an increasing number of children do not. Even when families can provide for basic needs, if there's not enough discretionary income, their ability to offer pre-school enrichment experiences equal to those affluent parents do as a matter of course is also impaired.

If you're working two jobs to put food on the table, how can you afford to buy the latest and greatest children's books, much less schedule the time to read with them at night? So what if the newest and best online games are available if you can't afford a computer or you live in a rural area where the internet access may still not be available? The show *Sesame Street* made a substantial difference in the lives of disadvantaged children for decades, but now the program will be broadcast over a premium channel for months before it appears on PBS. What if a parent can barely afford cable prices, much less HBO?

It's truly enriching for parents to expose their children to a Civil War battlefield or a museum of natural history, but what if "vacation" means parents stay home because they can't afford hotels?

Safety Needs: Crime and Violence

Physical, emotional, and sexual abuse, and another, even more insidious form—negligence—are epidemic, especially so in places where poverty is high and competition for having one's basic needs met is a daily occupation. All you have to do is turn on the news or hop on the internet.

We all agree that no child should have firsthand knowledge of rapes, murders, fights, and other forms of violence, much less learn to see them as "normal" in a civil society. They're traumatic for adults, let alone children. In the 20 years I have taught, more than a few students have told me that school is the only place they feel comfortable. A few have said they do not want to go home in the afternoon. Some cry when it is time for the holiday break or summer vacation because they don't know what will happen if they're home 24/7. And I'm expected to engage them in learning about cell parts, genetics, and ecological relationships so they can make a higher score on a standardized test?

At the same time, schools are increasingly *not* the safe places they used to be. As a teacher, I can't wave a magic wand and make it so. Within schools, the influence of bullying, racial clashes, and bigotry are ever-present. The effects of violence on the psyches of students, whether they're victims or observers of what happens to children in places like Newtown, cannot be ignored.

Social Needs

Familial Instability

From the advent of planes, trains, and automobiles and the growth of multi-state and multi-national corporations, our society has become increasingly transient. Most of us know or remember students in our classes whose parents took jobs in other cities and moved away or the reverse. Others, from military families, had lived all over the world, and upon the retirement of their fathers, had settled into a school.

Those students tell stories even now of the emotional effects of being uprooted from their friends, of the regular requirement that they adapt to a new place, a new school, new customs, new languages. But there was usually a good reason—their parents were transferred as they moved up in companies or the Army needed their specific talents somewhere else. With promotions came higher paychecks.

These families still exist, but there's a new sort of transient family for whom the social challenges persist. As poverty has increased and more families have become homeless, as more immigrants have come to America in search of safety and opportunity, the numbers of transient students have increased dramatically and the impact on children is debilitating. They've lost homes or immigrated from other countries where their lives were threatened.

Children in homeless families often move two and three times in the course of the same school year. Like immigrant families, they often live with first one friend or relative and then another, until they can establish themselves. Some families, buying into the "school choice" idea, move between schools in search of a school that fits their children's needs, often ignoring their need for stability first.

In short, what was once a fairly uncommon event has become commonplace. In Georgia, where I am, as many as 30% of students change schools each year. And I'm not talking about moving on from elementary school to middle school or from middle to high school. I'm talking about students who move multiple times during the same school year!

The impact on learning for those children is enormous. It's no wonder they fall behind. They are forced to adjust on a regular basis to new neighborhoods, new schools, new teachers, new friends. Being part of a group and feeling accepted as part of it is important to the development of a positive sense of self and identity. Traditionally, schools have provided a primary sense of belonging—the pride in and support of school sports teams is built on it. But for children who are constantly on the move, hope of belonging in a larger community disappears.

Racial/Ethnic Divisiveness

It's a known tendency that we often fear what we don't understand. And fear invokes in us the need to control it by avoiding, and diminishing the value of, the things that scare us. People of other races, cultures, ethnicities, faith traditions too often fall into those categories.

Some people maintain that racism and ethnic prejudices are things of the past, but what else do statements like the following, overheard at ballparks or other extracurricular events, mean, other than "I want my children to be around others like them"?

- "My child is white. I don't want him around all those blacks."
- "I want my Christian daughter around other Christians."
- "I make a lot of money. I don't want my kid around poor kids."
- "My son is smart—I don't want him in a class with kids who are dumber than he is."

No matter what race or culture we come from, it is perfectly natural to spend more time with those who seem more like us than those who are not. However, when the trend is to completely avoid those we perceive as different and deny them the same rights of citizenship, it is another thing altogether.

Although their original purpose was to allow some schools to operate under fewer externally-imposed rules, there is some evidence that the concept of "school choice" and the charter school movement have in some areas become symptomatic of this trend toward "separateness." This is reminiscent of the proliferation of thinly-veiled "private schools" that appeared across the Deep South on the heels of court-ordered desegregation in the 1960s (often referred to even today as "segregation academies.")

If any school's population is predominantly white, black, Muslim, Christian, Chinese, or based on any other ethnic, religious, or racial composition, the question of whether or not its underlying purpose is really localized segregation must be asked. The need to belong—in a family, in a school, in a community—transcends race, ethnicity, religion. If public schools are truly for all children, no policies that support racism, ethnic/religious prejudice, or classism—whether offered under the guise of school "choice" or lottery-based charter schools—have any place in the discussion.

Our new reality is that schools reflect our society, a compilation of multi-racial students from families of different levels of income and varied ethnic backgrounds and religious foundations. When education improvement is discussed, we cannot ignore the diverse socio-economic needs of our international, heterogeneous, socio-economically varied populations, but, above all, we cannot ignore the need to refoster a sense of community in society itself that transcends the demographic divisions between us.

Esteem Needs

Among the most misunderstood terms in use today is the concept of self-esteem. When Maslow spoke of the esteem needs, he spoke not of "feeling good about oneself," but of the intrinsic drive of all humans toward mastery and achievement in general—increasing knowledge of how the world works, growing confidence in our ability to provide for our own Level 1-3 needs (biological and physiological, safety and social needs), dreams of emulating others we admire, and the belief that with sufficient effort we can succeed in doing so. The result is a positive, yet realistic sense of self-esteem.

When I was a kid, my heroes were people like astronauts, actor John Wayne, even baseball player Bill Mazeroski. They were heroes, not because of the money they made or their looks but for what they accomplished. Astronauts faced death every time they rode in a rocket into space and explored the unknown. Although he was acting the part, John Wayne was a good guy who saved the heroine or arrested the bad guy. Bill Mazeroski, although he was a sports figure, hit the homerun in the bottom of the 9th inning to win the World Series.

My friends and I wanted to be like them—to do something adventurous, save the weak, or win the game. In addition to astronauts, actors and baseball players, we wanted to be scientists, engineers, businesspeople, firefighters, police officers, teachers—all respected professions that built and advanced our country or protected it. We wanted to identify with them, to contribute like them.

We used to pride ourselves in having a large middle class that could attain the American dream, which then most often meant having a good job or owning a home in which to raise our families. We used to pride ourselves in being the best of the best—in how our space program was superior to the then Soviet Union's. We had not just individual goals and aspirations, but national ones as well—a goal of defeating our adversaries in the Cold War before they took over the world.

I look at the nations whose student test scores are reported as higher than ours, such as China and India. They both have a rising middle class and space program. Their citizens have hope for the future—their version of the American dream. They are now where we were 50 years ago.

We've seen it since the beginning of our nation. Citizens of all varieties, with common goals and pride in achievement will work toward those goals together—even against what seem insurmountable odds—and succeed. The nation pulls together, people choose careers they believe contribute to the national goals as well as giving them the standard of living they aspire to. The feeling of working together to achieve a result that benefits all concerned is celebrated.

Erosion of Honor for Individual Merit

But, in America, and in many nations around the world, the definition of "hero" seems to have changed. The "war on terror" has not united Americans like WWII or the Cold War did. Goals today are far too often individual goals, separate from—and sometimes in direct opposition to—the goals of other citizens with rights equal to our own. Presidents Clinton, both Presidents Bush, and President Obama have all presented national goals in an effort to create a sense of common purpose, but none have taken hold as they once might have.

Part of the problem is that in a general way, the honor we once held for those who achieve academically has eroded, and with it the key to inspiring our children to want to be counted among them. On the other end of that problem is that we're not reinforcing those students who *do* work hard and achieve for their efforts. The connection between academic performance and the accolades that should come has fallen prey to what I call the **"Everyone Gets a Trophy"** syndrome.

The Everyone Gets a Trophy Syndrome

When my children played soccer, everyone on the team got a trophy. When my girls participated on swim teams, even 10th place got a ribbon. The awards table looked like a rainbow with all the color ribbons for all the places awarded. One of my daughters, when she was getting ready to move to her college dorm, asked me, "Why do I have so many trophies?" When I tried to explain that everyone got a trophy for participating, she said, "That's dumb. I should have only gotten a trophy if I did better than everyone else."

When did this happen?

My guess is that some of it began in the 80s when some child-rearing doctor somewhere said that a child's self-esteem was important, and everyone suddenly became self-proclaimed experts on the topic.

"Tell them they did good, even if they did not. Give them a 'U,' don't give them an 'F.' Don't hurt their feelings. Don't hold them back—or you'll hurt their self-esteem."

Propagation of this idea demonstrates a general failure to understand that the key to healthy self-esteem *is its basis in reality*. In other words, it is positive, realistic self-esteem based on actual achievement that's important. Just like my daughter, kids aren't stupid—they know when they have done their best and when they haven't. Unless we tie the rewards and accolades to doing one's best, we cannot ignite the motivation that fuels achievement in the first place.

By failing to connect effort and consequence, we create another problem—a heightened sense of entitlement. In other words, "inflated" self-esteem. Barry Switzer, a former college and NFL football coach is quoted as saying, "Some people are born on third base and think they hit a triple." Of such is the nature of entitlement—positive consequences with no connection to the effort that bring them about.

We've all heard some elected officials say that people who receive welfare eventually do not seek work because it is easier to get paid not to work. Congress regularly proposes budget cuts to reduce "entitlement" programs, such as food stamps, unemployment compensation, and "welfare" benefits. I get what they're saying, but I think a sense of entitlement has become entrenched in our culture at all levels of wealth. Companies are "entitled" to tax breaks in exchange for locating in a state. Farmers are criticized for subsidies, but giant agricultural co-ops claim and receive benefits for the same, and nobody says a thing.

When a student who gets a "B" or lower comes up to a teacher and says, "I deserve an A," or expresses honest surprise at failing a test, there's a problem. When a teacher gives a reward for a job well done to one student, and another who did not do his work complains, “That’s not fair,” there’s a problem. Many children are accustomed to getting whatever they want from their parents, family, and teachers, whether their behavior justifies it or not. If a football player doesn’t make the grade in science, should he pass because he’s important to the football team?

I think not, but we all know it happens.

Failure to teach (and reward) student responsibility

Most students do what is asked of them because they have been taught the unwritten rule that in school when a teacher (or any authority, for that matter) asks you to do something, you attempt to comply. By and large, children want to please their parents and teachers, and, as with any adult, they perceive that compliance with commands or requests is pleasing to their teachers. A much smaller group do the assignments because they know not doing it will impact their grades, and they know the importance of the grades to their future opportunities, and that they and only they will ultimately serve the consequences of their failure to perform.

But what about those students who seem just not to care? Teachers are asked to remind, ask, and make phone calls to parents to get late and missing assignments completed and turned in. When did it become a teacher’s responsibility to be sure a student gets all his or her work done? Students say they will do better when parent meetings occur (they’re still kids, remember), but then do nothing, and there are no negative consequences designed to stop the behavior from happening again.

In the workplace, the natural consequences of not doing what is required in the job are getting fired and losing your income. Forget to do your taxes? The wrath of the IRS falls upon you. Forget a spouse's birthday? The vitality of the relationship declines at the very least.

There are consequences, both positive and negative, for our actions. Knowing and experiencing those consequences, or seeing others experience them, helps us develop the skill of determining the path that will result in our greatest future success with the fewest unnecessary obstacles.

What are we teaching students who don't do their work and suffer no negative consequences? If a student doesn't appear to care about furthering his education, doesn't do the work required to get good grades or seek help when he's struggling, or is unconcerned about pleasing parents/teachers, at what point should a teacher abandon attempts to help him succeed? When does the responsibility for her education fall to the student? It's too late to wait until she's in college or in a paying job for her to discover what happens. Yet more and more children are oblivious to why they're even in school.

Intrinsic motivation and a sense of purpose

Like anyone else, kids must see a purpose in their education, and not just a general purpose—a purpose that impacts them personally, where they are and in terms of their developmental capacities to understand. Otherwise, it falls flat. Telling a first-grader that he needs to learn to read so he can go to college and get a good job accomplishes nothing. Connecting reading to stories about other children like him and experiences he's had is another thing. The college and good jobs "purpose" must wait.

But the point is still the same. To be motivated, we have to understand what we're striving for and believe that achieving it will result in something we aspire to. We need clearly defined goals that are rationally tied to that purpose. As with the macro goal of this book, in which we seek to define and agree on the purposes for public education, smaller "subgoals" must also be rationally tied to a purpose that transcends the goal itself, and communicated in ways people, even children, have the aptitude and development to understand.

And...we must ensure, especially in the early grades, that the rewards we give make sense—and are earned—and that the rewards we promise are the ones we deliver. Otherwise, we teach nothing except that we are confusing and untrustworthy.

Let's face it—life is often boring. But no matter how unentertaining a process, if we can keep our eyes on the *purpose* for whatever we are doing, we will go beyond the boredom, tedium, and minimum requirements and perform anyway. With apologies to the philosopher Nietzsche, "He who understands why he is doing something and agrees that he thinks it's a good thing can bear any how."

External rewards, however, even when consistent and rational, are not sufficient alone. The value of learning must become an intrinsic value. In other words, once a child reaches an age where the approval of parents and teachers (about age 12, generally) is declining in power as a reinforcement (external), the experience of learning must become more internal—not unlike the joy of learning we see in the two-year-old who crows at the discovery of his own power to throw his bowl of cereal across the room.

The fact that many kids seem not to know what to do with "free time," how to "entertain" themselves, is symptomatic of this disconnect. Their lives have been scheduled for them by their parents from day one—daycare, sports, play dates, piano practice and recitals—free play is foreign to many students. Parents send their children outdoors to play and they are at the door 20 minutes later wanting to come back in.

Just like other species—from lion cubs to puppy dogs—play and games are instinctual training grounds for life as an adult. We humans have an instinctual need to be connected with other humans, but technology has influenced us to depend on electronic connections over face-to-face interactions, even with family members. Unwittingly or otherwise, we have created a world of shorter and shorter attention spans and have taught our children that they are incapable of entertaining themselves.

As a result, many kids today expect to be entertained by their teachers. If not entertained, they act out, disrupting class, or say they are bored. I've actually had parents (and even administrators!) tell me that it is *my* responsibility to make the material I'm teaching less boring, with no recognition at all of their own accountability in not giving their children opportunity to be bored and discover alternatives for themselves. As a society, we seem to have conflated engagement with entertainment. The former is a two-way street, the latter something "done" to another. It is a teacher's job to *engage* not to entertain.

If we have to bribe, trick, entertain, and/or otherwise try to enhance the experience to get buy-in, it will not work. The connection between what we do in class and fulfillment of purpose is the only thing what will.

It is not an accident that more kids drop out between the 9th and 10th grades than at any other time. Nor is it a coincidence that one of the most frequent reasons given is the failure of education to connect the subject matter to the things that are important to them in "real life." Why? Because increasing numbers of students arrive in high school genuinely shocked to discover that *they* have responsibility and accountability for their own academic achievement and are consequently unprepared for the complexities of subject matter that await them. *And, for the most part, it isn't their fault.*

Having said that, it's clear that every generation of parents and teachers have said children were different from when they grew up. In the 60s and 70s, it was "rock and roll" that ruined them. In the 80s, the "Me" generation arrived. Next came the "X" generation, and more recently, the "Millenials." Life changes and moves forward. Music, clothes, hair styles, tattoos come and go. Different generations have different fads, interests, and/or favorites.

Though I'm increasingly concerned about what I'm seeing in the students who come to my classroom every day, let me hasten to say that many children are still active participants in the process of learning. They learn for the sake of learning or trust—even when they aren't completely sure what the purpose is—that what we teachers are talking about will be of some value to them at a later date. They are curious and compliant with school (and society's) rules and procedures.

I call those students "natural learners." They come to school ready to learn. They do their work, don't disrupt class, and are respectful. They have careers in mind, generally come from "successful" parents and see, to the extent they can, the benefits of a good school experience. Many of those students come from families who place education and achievement as a top priority.

Some of these children have personal obstacles to learning, such as language barriers and/or disabilities. They do not use the challenges as an excuse, but rather as a motivator, pushing themselves to succeed, because they see education as their ticket to a better life no matter what. I call these children "goal-oriented learners."

I am here to tell you, as one who sees them every day—180 days out of every year—that no child comes to school wanting to fail. Those who do well do so because they have already developed good work ethics and want to do the work because they see the connection between what they do in school and the trajectories of their futures. They do their work, are rewarded for it, and go on to live productive lives.

However, if when they arrive in our classes children expect to be given high grades they did not earn, be passed to the next grade even if they don't do the work, or experience no negative consequences for misbehavior, neither teachers nor administrators can change that mentality in 180 school days, especially when parents and politicians refuse to stand in support of them.

There have always been those who misbehave, who get into trouble, who fail to learn for a variety of reasons, and it is dangerous for us to generalize and label all children in sweeping ways, especially as it relates to education and achievement in general. It is even more dangerous to base policies and programs on the basis of the few, especially when we can't even agree on the sources of the problems themselves.

The bottom line is that teachers can only do so much. The social issues impacting our ability to do the jobs we are now required to do *cannot be addressed by educators alone.* The expectation of positive change requires that those with control over what happens are made responsible for the outcomes. Teachers can't control whether a child eats, sleeps, is safe at home or on the internet. We can't control whether the economy improves, where higher-paying jobs will be found. We can't instill a sense of wonder about the world and a sense of purpose in children in the face of the social ills that confront us as a nation.

Only when those with the power to solve those problems work with us to change them will educators be able to do the crucial jobs we were hired and trained to do.

Chapter 5
Pressures Inside the Schools

As we talked about in the previous chapter, there are a number of social pressures outside the classroom that impact the ability of teachers to do their primary jobs. But the reality is that until those with the wherewithal to lead in relieving some of those social pressures take action, nothing will change. If we realistically expect to even come close to achieving the desired outcomes we say we seek, schools will be forced to intervene. Some are already trying to.

"Free" Lunch

School nutrition programs are one service that I think about often. In the beginning, they were a service provided primarily for two reasons: 1) in response to the malnourishment of many children in urban environments across the country, stimulated in part by a book, *Poverty*, written in 1904, which first focused widely on the effect of malnourishment on the mental capacities of children, and 2) because, secondary to the influence of increased populations, children were required to travel further from home than ever to attend school.

Whereas it had previously been common for students in both urban neighborhoods and rural communities to go home for lunch, the practice was no longer possible. The provision of a noon-day meal, for some, eventually became a convenience so that parents would not have to make their children's lunch every day. It was easier just to pay for the service.

First supported by private institutions and municipalities, the responsibility for underwriting the costs of school lunches soon passed to the local school districts, where, for the most part, they remain, mandated and supported now through state and federal programs. Today, school lunch programs, also known as school nutrition programs, are embedded in the everyday expectations of citizens, but so are the original drivers that led to schools providing lunch to students in the first place.

The need for the "free and/or reduced" lunch program financial supplements is as broad as ever. The federal government sends billions of dollars to schools to pay for lunches that families cannot afford to make or buy for their child. Families have to apply for the program and are screened for need but the poverty rate seems to have skyrocketed, so that free/reduced lunches are provided to an overwhelming number of students in schools across the country—inner city, suburban, and rural districts alike.

School lunch programs have reportedly become a primary source of food for many children in this country. Not only are schools providing for the noon-day meal, but adding free/reduced breakfasts to students at an alarming rate. And, in some communities, schools and nonprofit organizations are supplying breakfast and lunch to children even while school is out of session—in the summers and over holidays.

I am not against feeding children—they need food if they are not eating at home. But the question needs to be asked: Why do the schools need to be the primary source of food for so many children? Has feeding students become part of the social contract between schools and the general public? If so, then as stakeholders in the success outcomes we demand, we must accept the responsibility for underwriting the costs associated.

Social Services

In addition to nutrition programs, social services programs are also increasingly moving into schools.

School counseling programs have expanded beyond what I could have ever imagined when I was in school. Years ago, the responsibility of guidance counselors were to intervene with children when their grades fell, they had boy/girl issues, or in the rare situations of their parents divorcing and other family issues.

Counselors still do these things, but there many more divorces and some are pretty nasty. I can't count the number of children I have taught whose grades have suddenly dropped, they quit participating in class, and they seemed distracted more than usual for a middle-school-aged kid—and I came to find out their parents were going through a divorce. Mom and Dad are fighting over custody and the child has heard what they are saying about each other. I've even received requests from parents wanting information on how their child is performing and acting in school, only to find out they want to use the information as evidence in court for how the other parent is failing in their duties and why they should have custody.

Counselors today console children who have a parent who is suffering in some way or perhaps dying. They solicit donations of basic school necessities for children—things like notebook paper, pencils, and book bags. They hold fundraisers for funds to help families with everything from home furnishings to rent to other basic needs at home, all to help the children in their schools have some sense of stability for a short time at school.

In short, the role of counselors has expanded, but they aren't alone. All school employees—teachers, bus drivers, custodial workers, administrators—are required, by state law, to notify our supervisors if we see what may be evidence of abuse—physical and sexual—and they are then required to notify the appropriate legal authorities.

I am in favor of the requirement, but alarmed at what seems to be an increasing trend. It tears my heart out to see and hear stories of children I have taught afraid to go home on the school bus at the end of the day because they are victims of sexual assault or recipients of physical beatings from caregivers who are violent alcoholics or otherwise mentally ill.

As with the increased need for basic nutrition, when social workers are housed in the schools, it is a signal that something is wrong outside the schools. Yet, as the institutions in closest daily contact with students, for the near future, schools must remain on the front line for detection and action.

Medical Care

Since I was in school, what were simply places to go for a band-aid or an aspirin have morphed into mini-emergency rooms and doctor's offices. There may be an RN at the district office who guides and directs clinic operations at the school, or the school "nurse" may not be a nurse at all. Instead, the job may be held by school clerks who have no medical background and are hired at clerk's wages, trained in basic first aid, and then expected to be the first responders for major medical emergencies at the school.

They're exposed to viruses, bacteria, and blood every day. Parents who work often send their children to school when the child should probably stay at home, but their jobs prohibit them from taking the day off or to do so will result in docked wages. If a parent can't get off work, the "clinic lady" houses them on a make shift bed or sends them back to class—possibly spreading the virus or bacteria. If a child is hit in the head and knocked unconscious during PE, the "clinic lady" is called immediately for help.

Then there are all the medicines that must be managed every day—medications for ADD and ADHD, maintenance and emergency inhalers for asthma, insulin injections for children with diabetes, antibiotics, anti-psychotics, you name it. Make one mistake and the consequences could be devastating.

Again, I am not against schools taking on this role, but it should be performed by certified healthcare personnel—not school clerks—and the salary funded at a level commensurate with that commanded by other healthcare personnel at a similar level.

And to make matters worse, schools are not only required to fulfill basic needs, but are asked to compile reports for legislators at will, on whatever happens to be the issue of the day. In my school, the PE teachers have been tasked with conducting fitness reports and sending them home in report cards, as well as to the state for compilation of statistics about the fitness of the children in the state. The counselors are required to conduct surveys with students about their exposure and/or use of tobacco, prescription drugs, alcohol, illegal drugs, home situations, and many other topics.

I understand why schools are asked to conduct the surveys. As with virtually anything else, as we've seen, it is because we are public education and see the children every day. If we need to track the information, which is questionable from the outset, it won't likely get done anywhere else. But it is one more thing that dilutes the focus of schools and impedes achievement of the outcomes we say we demand.

After-School "Daycare"

There have always been before- and after-school programs for tutoring, clubs, and athletics, but increasingly, more programs seem geared toward little more than supervised child care. Some programs are designated as remediation and enrichment programs, but I venture to guess that many are established because many children would be sent home to empty houses or apartments. Again, public education has stepped in to try and provide for a social need it is not prepared to fulfill.

Summary

The primary responsibility of schools and teachers, that of creating an environment conducive to learning, once only applied to the environment inside the buildings built for that purpose and that purpose alone.

All of the things I have mentioned so far are symptoms of a far greater issue. In the larger sphere, we need to do some self-reflecting not just with regard to the environment in schools but the total environment in which our children are growing up today.

Are we going to hold public education responsible for addressing not only the issues of academic performance, but of providing food, mental health services, medical clinics, and childcare? Then we had better be ready to acknowledge that if "schools are failing," it is because society in general is failing to provide for the basic needs of an increasing majority of children—things they must have to survive—long before they walk through a classroom door.

Chapter 6
Pressures Inside the Classroom

The pressures aren't just applied from the outside, however. Some of the greatest pressures are applied from within. Among them are larger class sizes, an overemphasis on grades as a measure of success rather than subject mastery, and something we've already talked about and will talk about more—high stakes testing.

Larger class sizes

I teach seventh grade. When I started teaching 20 years ago, I averaged 22–24 students per science class (92 in a day). I now average 31–33 students per science class (124 in a day). I have friends in other middle schools who have 36–38 in their science classes. One friend who teaches high school history has 38 students in his classes (185 students in a day)!

Gifted and AP (Advanced Placement) classes used to have ceilings for how many students could be in the class in the range of 17-20, which provided opportunities for teachers to give more individualized instruction.

But, in many school systems, those caps have been removed, and classes have upwards of 30–34 students.

Why the changes? That's fairly simple to answer—class sizes have increased because of budget shortages and cuts in funds allotted for teachers' salaries. On paper, it's simple math—the same numbers of students with fewer teachers equals more students per teacher. But the impacts of increased class sizes aren't a math problem and they aren't simple.

I have heard the debates. I have seen that "research says" fewer than 15 students is the optimum number in a class. And I've heard it said that once over 15, the number of students in a classroom really doesn't matter, because a "good" teacher will be able to teach them. But rather than go into "what research says," I can only share my own personal experiences with increased class sizes.

This may sound odd, but the fact that the "high stakes test scores" have risen in my state the last five years alarms me. Higher test scores are a good thing, but the part that scares me is the fact that, lacking information or judgment about what constitutes "learning," the majority of legislators see the rise in scores and justify their budget cuts. It's too easy to assume that larger class sizes have no impact on learning, when what's actually happening makes it increasingly less likely that we can achieve the larger goals outlined in Chapter 3.

It is also a concern of mine that legislators and budget committees will look at high stakes testing results, see that scores have increased and make judgments that schools don't need funding restored to pre-2008 levels.In their minds, the schools are obviously doing "well" and in some cases better with the smaller budgets—based on that erroneous idea that schools are like businesses and children are like widgets. Unfortunately, like many teachers, I know that scores haven't increased because students have mastered the material, but for other reasons that are actually counterproductive.

In my view, two factors contribute to scores going up. The first is that we have been getting the message to "do more with less" and, as dedicated professionals, we upped our efforts to help the kids do better. But I am hearing more and more teachers saying they cannot keep up this pace much longer. They are burning out.

A friend and fellow teacher and I recently talked about "super teachers" such as Jamie Escalante in the movie "Stand and Deliver," Erin Gruwell in "Freedom Writers," and others about whom movies were made to laud their accomplishments. The movies show how they took students from poverty and those facing great barriers to successful achievement. The movies show the costs to their personal lives. But what the movies do *not* tell is that "super teachers" burn out after four or five years and move out of teaching into other roles. It is not realistic to expect someone to maintain that level of energy expenditure for long periods. Those teachers gave themselves totally to their students, and they paid a price. Their success was ultimately at the expense of their personal lives. As mentioned earlier, in the 19th and early 20th centuries, teachers were often unmarried and without families and other responsibilities of their own, but that is no longer the case, nor do I believe it should be.

The second and more compelling reason I think kids are doing better on high stakes tests is that teachers have figured out how to prepare kids for the tests—by providing "drill and kill" study guides, review sheets, and time spent discussing test-taking strategies. There's no doubt that we know how to prepare kids for the tests better than we did 10 years ago, but we also know that the results of shifting our focuses away from teaching to test-score boosting will come with some dreadful costs that we are already seeing.

For example, increased class sizes have forced me to change how I approach teaching in order to fulfill basic curriculum requirements. With 24 students, I used to do more science labs, and regularly assigned projects that required kids to present their results in front of the class. This gave them practice in speaking in front of groups, as well as giving me a chance to evaluate their understanding of the material. To do that with more kids means more time presenting, which cuts into the time I have to introduce new material.

Sandwich that with the increase in the actual numbers of standardized testing days, and overall, I have far fewer days to actually teach. I don't want to "sacrifice" days to presentation versus days of "active learning" lessons like science labs, but I do.

With increased class sizes, too, I deal with more behavior issues. When kids are packed into rooms, they are, by default, closer in physical proximity to each other, which makes for increased talking. With more children, the odds of the occasional major "disruptor" also increases.

The added energy I must expend just to manage my class frankly wears me out. I go home more tired than I used to. The more kids I have to monitor every period each day, the more discipline issues I have to deal with, the more papers I have to grade, the more parent contacts I have to make to discuss discipline and academic issues. I am exhausted when I go home, to the point that I don't have the energy for my family and personal activities I once treasured.

In the classroom, I can't learn the names of the good kids as quickly as I used to. Instead of 92 names, I now have 124 to learn and remember. I learn the names of the disruptive ones, the needy ones, and the ones who answer all the questions long before I learn the quiet, studious, and "does whatever they are told" kids. There have been times in October—three months into school—when the principal asked me if a kid was in my class and I was embarrassed to admit that I didn't know without looking at the class roll.

Overemphasis on grades

In their original form, grades were simply a way to show progress in student learning. But a single number or letter cannot adequately convey what's going on with an individual child. There are too many variables, influences—qualitative factors that grades do not and, frankly, can't show.

I understand the need for grades, but in our drive for simplifying everything, we often look for a single measure that sums up whatever the topic. A grade is high or low, good or bad—there's no room for gray. As I mentioned in Chapter 2, sports teams are either "winners" or "losers" based on the win/loss stats. Friends, neighbors, strangers are labeled "good" or "bad" based on single events. We have become an excessively judgmental society, one that no longer tolerates or perhaps understands the complexity of the systems we have created. The entire state of public education has been reduced to the sum total of a number. Once again, we have lost touch with the purpose grading systems were put into place to measure. The two most important questions we should be asking: "Does research support that what we are measuring actually predicts success based on how we define success?" and "Are we measuring what we think we're measuring?"

Children who receive high grades may be showing they've mastered the material presented or that they've have "learned" to anticipate what will be on an upcoming test and memorize it. Generally speaking, a low grade can mean that a child has *not* learned what he or she was supposed to, but in today's school environment, it is equally possible that he learned some of the required material but didn't study for a test or turn in assignments. Or, perhaps he missed class because of sickness or homelessness. Then again, he may have a learning disability that hasn't been diagnosed.

Add to that the fact that every state and school district has different standards that denote "mastery." For instance, if a "D" fulfills the requirement for promotion, what does an "A" signify? Most classes now give pre- and post-tests to measure student "growth." If a student gets a score of at least a "D" on the pre-test, according to some districts, wouldn't that mean the student has already met the standard?

A better question might be, "How do we determine if the material on the pre- and post-tests adequately measures what we want a child to learn?" What other less-easy-to-measure intangibles are there that a student must experience and demonstrate in order to truly show "growth"? Above and beyond the basic purpose of grades showing whether or not the child learned the required material for the semester or year, are we measuring the acquisition of other skills that will benefit the child in his future life?

If you're a teacher, have you ever had a parent or student ask for extra credit to bring up a grade or offered it for the same reason? What is the purpose of extra credit? To give students another chance to do something that they didn't do the first time? Does it add value to the child's learning? Or is it just a way to add points by "doing something" to increase the grade, like paying to upgrade a seat on an airplane?

Some of my most memorable personal lessons came from when I screwed up and had to take responsibility for it. When I screwed up in class, at work, or at home, I remembered it the next time I was confronted with a similar situation. In today's grading schemes, are we teaching children that it is okay to mess up because someone will always come along and fix it for you?

Though some may think it a good thing, in my opinion, we are doing our students a disfavor. Too many young workers seem to be surprised when they get a job and when they don't do their work right the first time, the consequences are much more severe than they've come to expect. In the real world, there are few second chances and virtually never third and fourth and fifth chances. Supervisors don't give employees "extra credit" opportunities to help them keep a job.

I have talked to many corporate leaders and friends who are business owners who say they no longer look at grades when hiring employees. Instead, they want students who are persistent, have good work ethics, and can communicate effectively both orally and in writing. The knowledge and skills they specifically need to be successful in the job, they report, will be taught to them on the job.

They tell me there is no way schools can teach students all of the specialized information they'll need to complete the jobs they will have, and that they would rather hire a hard worker with less than stellar grades than a straight-A student who can't seem to get to work on time.

Are we teaching how to learn material that isn't needed for most jobs and not teaching the very skills that *are* needed, like the ability to think, to weigh options, to set goals and create coherent plans to achieve them? If the primary stated outcome of public education is to prepare students for the workplace, isn't the breakdown a systemic one that requires of teachers (and punishes them for failure to teach) something that isn't relevant to the very outcomes we seek?

Parents, teachers, politicians, and the media want a grade, a finite numerical value to assign to a child and they want that number to mean the exact same thing with respect to every district, every teacher, every student. But no one is asking the question, "At what point in our lives and careers are test-taking skills of any value?"

Retention as help or punishment?

I have read many articles, opinions, and research papers on the effect of holding kids back when they're not ready. There's no pat answer because the circumstances contributing to a child's failure to achieve vary, and retaining a kid can have variable impacts on self-esteem. In short, some kids would benefit from another year, and some would not. But I think the age of the child is an important criterion.

The development of identity and self-esteem begins in earnest around age six or seven. Our ability to influence whether a child develops positive or negative self-esteem in school is much greater at this point than at any other.

Although I teach middle school students, it seems to me that especially in the early grades, focusing on which skills need shoring up for an individual student is more important than what grade he is in when the resources are made available to him. The negative emotional and social impacts of not moving up with other kids in his same grade level will have longer lasting effects. A six-year-old won't understand why she's not being moved—all she'll know is that for some reason, she isn't "good enough." A high school student, on the other hand, is capable of understanding the connection between cause and effect, even if he doesn't see it.

The Testing Process

Students have always taken "local exams" like end-of-unit tests so that their teachers can determine if they learned the material required by the standards. There are a number of types of tests that traditionally have been used to assess learning—multiple choice questions, fill-in-the-blanks, true/false items, essays, performance-based "tests" like labs.

Another fallout from increased class sizes is that the more students one has, the longer it takes to grade tests, which has caused many of us to rely more and more only on multiple-choice tests rather than the full range of test items once used.

Let's do the math. If it takes four minutes to read and grade two essays on a test, the change from 92 kids to 124 means it would take me an extra two hours to grade a test that included written essays. And that doesn't even account for the extra time required to grade projects or homework assignments, or deal with discipline issues.

Another rampant phenomenon is the mandate that students be allowed to retake tests if they don't pass in the first place. I see two negative ramifications:

1. Some students take tests to see what's on them, fail them on purpose, and then take them again. The teacher in the classroom next to mine told me she was returning test papers and overheard a student complain because he made a 70. (The "retake policy" applies to grades 69 and below.)
2. We do students an injustice by teaching them that if you don't pass the first time, you can always do it again. I literally heard an adult misread the teleprompter on live television and then say, "I want a redo." Chances are we won't be seeing him again.

In either case, we reinforce the idea and expectation that there's no reason to give your best efforts the first time around. There will always be another chance to do your best. The first year "retests" were allowed in the high school where my wife Loretta taught, a future valedictorian came to take a retest in her class. "It's not fair to the other students who properly prepared for the test," said the student, "and it makes me a poorer student, because it gives me a reason not to study as hard the first time."

And now there are "study guides." With increasing regularity, parents request (and some districts require) teachers to provide study guides for upcoming tests as if everything else done in the classroom is for naught. (Going to class and paying attention was all the study guide I, and most of my contemporaries, had.) Back to the message that high test scores alone are the most important outcome desired.

Something has changed dramatically if students require the spoon feeding of study "guides." Studying and learning, which is the point of studying, after all, includes taking notes in class, reviewing them regularly during the course of a unit or semester, and actually *doing* homework assignments designed to reinforce retaining the important details and concepts of the subject matter involved. Is it possible that we have raised an entire generation of students who have no idea how to study?

The combination of increased class sizes and an emphasis on high stakes testing in the last 15–20 years has reduced learning to preparing to regurgitate answers on multiple-choice tests, not just for high stakes tests but for every test. That's because teachers like me no longer have the time or energy to adequately assess student progress and because many schools pressure teachers to pass everyone.

What are the effects on the children themselves? High anxiety, pressure to perform on tests irrelevant to the workplace they face, and an absence of opportunity to learn the crucial skills that *are* relevant not just for the workplace but in life.

How did this happen? Well, for starters, our governments and the media have had an awful lot to do with it.

Chapter 7
The Effects of Politics, Sports and the Media on Public and Parental perceptions

Overall, most citizens of the United States are balanced in their approaches and able to look at all sides of an issue. As I mentioned before, depending on the survey, about 80% of parents and children report that they are happy with their schools and teachers. So who's driving the negative conversation?

Schools, whether public or private, are based within a community of people, and as such, reflect the social and cultural norms and expectations/beliefs of the individuals in those communities. We know that schools in upper-class communities with educated and involved parents tend to perform better than those in poverty-stricken areas with uneducated and uninvolved parents and caregivers.

Of course, some kids will rise or fall regardless of their location, but the criticisms of schools tend to be generalized from community to community, ignoring the differences between those communities. When people blame schools for the ills of education, they are in reality blaming the communities around them and society's failure to support a level playing field. The task to educate naturally falls to government to ensure, but the authority to do that does not include management of the day-to-day process of teaching, because legislators are not skilled in educating students and can't speak with any knowledge or intelligence about what should happen in a classroom. It is dangerous indeed for the future of our country to depend on the hyperbolic rhetoric of political campaigns, and yet that's where we find ourselves.

A Nation at Risk

Upon his election, the Reagan Administration sought to reverse President Carter's establishment of the Department of Education as a cabinet-level position, and succeeded in stripping education of much of the funding allocated by the Congress at the time of the department's establishment.

It was what would come next, though, that would start the ball rolling and create an overwhelmingly adversarial attitude toward public education.

There's no doubt that education has, from the time of Benjamin Franklin forward, been a political football, but the game escalated exponentially in 1983 when the results of the landmark study "A Nation at Risk" was published. Rather than paraphrase the document, the introductory paragraph is reproduced on the next page.

An Open Letter to the American People:

A Nation at Risk

An Imperative for Education Reform

1983

"Our Nation is at risk. Our once unchallenged preeminence in commerce, industry, science, and technological innovation is being overtaken by competitors throughout the world. This report is concerned with only one of the many causes and dimensions of the problem, but it is the one that undergirds American prosperity, security, and civility. We report to the American people that while we can take justifiable pride in what our schools and colleges have historically accomplished and contributed to the United States and the well-being of its people, the educational foundations of our society are presently being eroded by a rising tide of mediocrity that threatens our very future as a Nation and a people. What was unimaginable a generation ago has begun to occur—others are matching and surpassing our educational attainments. If an unfriendly foreign power had attempted to impose on America the mediocre educational performance that exists today, we might well have viewed it as an act of war."

(To see the entire document, go to: http://www.ed.gov/pubs/NatAtRisk/index.html)

Once again, as with the Department of Education and the Elementary and Secondary Education Act, the stated intent of the study would be totally overrun. Instead of pushing education to adjust to the new realities after a hundred years of formal education in the USA, the alarmist tone of the title and the very first sentence set into motion an over-reaction that has resulted in 30+ years of misguided judgment from self-designated experts, partisan divides, and in terms of reform, nothing of substance.

Once they were successful in communicating to the public that there was a crisis beyond measure in public education, politicians have used this manufactured crisis as a pawn to get votes. And by creating a problem and then convincing their constituents that a crisis existed, they secured their own positions by promising "fixes" for the phantom problem. And now, ***they may well have brought a real problem into being.***

In reality, a single elected official has very little influence on what happens in the classroom except perhaps in supporting or opposing legislative mandates with respect to teacher salaries and loads placed on the shoulders of teachers. At the core, however, is what I alluded to in Chapter 2 with respect to the application of the laws of supply and demand and market competition to public schools.

In terms of the expected output, schools aren't businesses. If we follow the ideas of the free market and its tenets to their conclusions, it is obvious why they can't apply to education. Children are not widgets. The "raw materials" of the school system are *not* equivalent, in any sense of the word, to those used in a manufacturing plant, and the methods employed to increase productivity DO NOT APPLY.

Why not? *Because teachers don't create products for the general masses.*

Pour liquid metal or plastic into a mold and it generally comes out in a predefined form. If the raw materials meet the standards of quality recognized in the industry of choice, they can be consistently manipulated into inanimate products or services that all come out looking exactly like the engineering specifications and each other.

But children are not inanimate objects. They are not "empty heads" that we open up and pour knowledge and skills into. They are not products we move along, in locked step, on an assembly line. Every student in every school is a living, breathing human being with a unique brain, a unique family situation, a unique socio-economic status, unique aptitudes and disabilities, unique languages, and unique personalities—all of which have profound effect on attention, motivation, and ultimately the acquisition of knowledge and skill.

The result of the political drive to "fix" education using principles of the free market is a primary contributor to the proliferation of the "quality control" procedure known as high stakes testing. As with sales quotas, the model assumes that achievement can be measured and transformed into numbers and ranks.

In line with the misguided idea that children are widgets, agencies tasked with overseeing "quality control" have developed standardized curriculum that can be tested, easily quantified, put into categories, and compared (in other words, multiple-choice tests). It might be effective if the goal of education was to create "Stepford" children resembling boxes of cereal. But it isn't.

Teachers know that "bubble sheet" answers can reflect only the fact-driven lower-level thinking skills of Bloom's Taxonomy, the scale teachers have used successfully since the late 1950s to plan lessons for their students. In both, memorization and recall of facts is the first stage of learning.

But true learning ***doesn't stop there***. Unless comprehension of concepts and understanding of how those facts relate to other facts and concepts occur, no skill in applying what is learned to actually solve real life problems—in the workplace or otherwise—is acquired. The upper levels of the taxonomy require even more complex thinking and cannot be quickly and easily evaluated using standardized testing, which it takes only common sense to see. To assess if learning has occurred requires written essays, verbal reports, labs, and/or presentations, which simply cannot be achieved with the numbers of students being evaluated or the methods employed.

Seasoned teachers, administrators, and professional educators at all levels are well aware of this fact, but mandates arrive from legislators, governors, Congress, and the president—intended only to meet their politically-based purposes. Performance evaluations and the livelihoods of those teachers are therefore not dependent upon what they know to be relevant, but on the whims of officials with no obvious understanding of what education entails. Anyone honestly surprised at the recent cheating scandals in Atlanta and other areas is either incapable of "higher order" thinking or is not in contact with reality.

Adding to the intensity of pressure from political motivations, each level of government contributes funds to the local schools so each has a "voice" in what happens. And yet, the only experts on the current state of education—classroom teachers—are *not* elected officials and seldom have control over or input into the funding decisions made.

We teachers are excluded from political conversations that have substantive impacts on our ability to do the jobs we—and we alone—have been explicitly trained to do. Instead, the conversation is driven by parents, politicians, and business leaders who perceive themselves to be experts on education. Nothing of substance can or will result as long as teachers are denied input.

The Real Legacy of "No Child Left Behind"

As noted before, "No Child Left Behind" (NCLB) was not a new act of Congress when President Bush signed it into law in 2002. The last renewal of the Act, known as "Every Student Succeeds Act," (signed into Law December 10, 2015), makes changes that respond to some of the issues of "No Child Left Behind," but the legacy of the Act will take years to undo. The title alone speaks to the politics of education.

The five basic goals for NCLB were as follows:

1. All students will reach high standards by 2013 - 2014, attaining proficiency or better in reading and mathematics.
2. All limited English proficient students will reach high academic standards, proficiency or better in reading, language arts, and mathematics.
3. All students will be taught by highly qualified teachers by 2005-2006.

4. All students will be educated in environments that are safe, drug free, and conducive to learning.
5. All students will graduate from high school.

Let's take a look at each of the goals and what *actually* happened.

1. All students will reach high standards by 2013-2014, attaining proficiency or better in reading and mathematics.

The basic premise of this section implied that "every child would be successful in school by the end of 2014 (i.e., no one would fail).

The population of the USA is made up of people with all levels of abilities and competencies. The "normal curve" associated with many of those abilities and competencies suggests that they are scattered along a continuum, with the majority in the middle, and smaller numbers stretching to the extremes above and below. By default, a certain number have always fallen below a line of "proficiency" with respect to reading and mathematics and likely always will. In other words, to suggest that "no one would be left behind, i.e., fail, was an impossible goal from the outset.

So what was the impact of this goal of the NCLB? Coupled with its requirement that high stakes testing be used as a measurement of whether or not a school achieved this inherently impossible goal, administrators were forced to shift emphasis away from the tried-and-true standard teaching techniques to strategies for increasing scores for lower level students to one of "minimal competency."

Not only that, but state departments of education began to set the described "proficiency" level lower on their state tests, lower even than what had traditionally been seen as a "D" level. Teachers felt the pressure to make sure the slower students were able to pass the tests, often at the expense of using their energies to focus on educating their other students.

History may prove that by 2014, even more children were "left behind" than ever before. In any case, attempts to achieve this goal resulted in benefits only to politicians.

2. All limited English proficient students will reach high academic standards, proficiency or better in reading, language arts, and mathematics.

I agree that, like any other students, those with limited English capabilities should reach high academic standards. But too many people are focused on whether immigrants will learn English. They fail to account for the impact of including the scores of ESL students along with those for which English is native.

Our country is a country of immigrants. Since the beginning, it has been obvious that to perform in traditionally higher paying jobs requires that especially the firstborn generations learn English. But implementation of this goal and unreasonable expectations for the time period during which English was required to be learned caused many schools to be labeled as "Not Meeting Adequate Yearly Progress (AYP)." For example, because of a handful of 15 non-English-speaking students out of 2,600 in a school where I once taught, the school was judged as failing to demonstrate AYP on the language arts portion of the state tests.

Of course, those students had difficulty passing tests in English! They had just moved to America and hadn't had time to gain command of their new language.

But, when their scores, lumped in with all others, meant the school hadn't met AYP, the community, media, and politicians generalized and interpreted the results to mean the school was failing. This, despite the fact that 2,585 students had demonstrated success.

3. All students will be taught by highly qualified teachers by 2005-2006.

There is no doubt that teachers should be held accountable as in any other job (skilled or unskilled), but accountability must be paired with authority to control outcomes and the standards of performance must be relevant to success in the job and evaluation in the hands of people familiar with the demands of the job. The NCLB said that if a teacher was not "highly qualified," he or she should not be permitted to teach.

In the first place, the law did not provide a clear definition for "highly qualified," nor were those who wrote the law "highly qualified" to do so.

By 2005, for practical reasons, this part of the law was "relaxed" or ignored, but the basic idea that too many teachers are incompetent had already been planted in the minds of the public.

As there are in all professions, including politicians, the reality is that there have always been poor, average, and highly-qualified teachers. To suggest that the majority of teachers aren't "highly qualified" is not only insulting but borders on thin contact with reality.

4. All students will be educated in environments that are safe, drug free, and conducive to learning.

I agree with our striving for an ideal of providing a safe, non-disruptive environment for students. I want our children to attend safe and drug-free schools with an environment conducive to learning. It is clear that, as a Maslow Hierarchy Level 2 need, a feeling of safety is crucial to learning. But providing an emotionally safe environment in a classroom is not the same as guarding the perimeter of a school.

Teachers and school administrators are not and should not bear the whole responsibility of ensuring safety for students. Control that any school or teacher has over safety outside the school environment is variable at best, despite their school's attempts to provide for other non-academic problems like food, mental health, and medical care.

It is the responsibility of the communities in which the schools exist to provide an environment in which teachers can, with a minimum of interference from the outside, do the jobs they have always done well.

5. All students will graduate from high school.

I agree that the goal of 100% graduation rate is good and something we should strive for. However, the reality is that all students are different with varying needs, interests, circumstances, and goals for life and the standard high school model of preparing students for college *does not fit all students.* If we truly expect to achieve 100% graduation rates, we need to provide alternatives for those children and youth who do not—or cannot practically at the time—aspire to the traditional college environment.

My wife Loretta, who retired this year, taught a high school "college prep" class, Political Systems. She once had a student we'll call Curt, who spent most of his time with his head down, asleep. He seemed to hate the prospect of learning anything, because despite her persistent efforts to engage him, with support from his father, the sleeping in class continued, and he eventually failed.

Later, Loretta took another class to an open house at a technical school associated with the high school. As they approached one of the exhibits, she was stunned to see none other than Curt, smiling and handing out flyers about another class he was taking. She left the open house convinced that had she been able to present the topic of political systems in the context of Curt's obvious technical interests, his behavior in class would have been quite different. For the traditional college-bound student, the connection between the subject matter and future coursework required of them in pursuit of a college degree was fine. For a student like Curt, it was not. It wasn't that he hated learning—it was that *he saw no connection between that information and the future he saw for himself.*

The re-introduction of non-college tracks is not "dumbing down the program," as some would suggest. Instead, it would mean changing to meet the needs of our diverse student populations and communities, and those of both the skilled and unskilled sectors of the workplace. Match the skill and the content of the education to the eventual plan, e.g. make clear the *purpose*, and then we will see high school graduation rates increase.

The "Every Student Achieves Act"

Finally, after almost ten years, reauthorization of the Elementary and Secondary School Act came to pass on December 10, 2015. There were many factors, forces, influences, and power struggles that had to be overcome but Congress finally succeeded in overcoming them in conference committee (the House and Senate versions had some major differences between them).

At the time of this writing, it is too soon to speak to the impacts, positive or negative, of the "Every Student Achieves Act" so my comments will be left at the historical influence of "No Child Left Behind" for now. I am hopeful that now a real dialogue can occur to improve public education using the framework of the new law and that the dialogue involves people working together to improve education, rather than to promote their own personal agendas and special interests.

We shall see.

Sports in the Schools

During the last century, sports have played an important part, not just in society, but specifically in the educational realm. There's no doubt about the lessons that can be learned regarding teamwork, dealing with the emotions of winning and losing, and pride in the school community itself.

I played sports while in school. The neighborhood kids used to come to my house (or me to theirs), knock on the door and ask if I could come out and play baseball. We played with anyone who was home that day or didn't have chores to do.

When I got to junior high (7th grade), the schools had organized sports, so I signed up for football and track, and then soccer in high school. There were three seasons and kids picked one or more and then moved on to the next sport. Sports were fun and they attracted some kids to school who might not have been there, but they were *extra-curricular*, not the primary focus.

In many schools, today, however, sports have become a dominant force. In some, the main source of pride is how well the football or basketball teams perform. Athletes are treated with much more attention and accolade than non-athletes—local newspapers seldom publish the "super six" science, math, language arts, Spanish, or social studies students.

Schools pay their sports coaches stipends for the time and energy they spend preparing and taking their athletes to competitions, but academic team sponsors often receive nothing at all. A freshman soccer assistant coach gets money to coach, even though she may be doing it because no one else would, while a teacher with a passion for academics may prepare her students for four months for a mock trial competition but receives no financial incentive.

Yet, the variety of academic subject areas opens doors for far more of our children than sports ever can. In 20 years of teaching, I have had a handful of students receive sports-related scholarships to Division I schools. In 20 years, I have had one student make an NFL team (Atlanta Falcons). And yet, in those 20 years, when I've asked students in my 7th grade class what they want to be when they grow up, far more than a handful are invested in becoming professional sports stars, despite the odds against that. We are doing those students who play sports an injustice, because the academics will take the great majority of them further ahead in life than their sports ever will.

The Media

Further reinforcing the over-emphasis of sports are the media moguls. When, for example, have you read in a major newspaper the names of the colleges or universities the top 20 students of a class were going to attend?

I want to hear where the students in my community chose to attend college because they will be the professionals, specialists, technicians and active contributors to the future of my community and state. Who chose Yale, the state university, Armed Forces academies, or technical colleges? I want to know about the people who will be fixing the leaks in my plumbing, drawing blood from my arm at the doctor's office, paying taxes, and supporting my community. Don't you?

Every news event becomes a hyper-event, disaster, drop-everything story. Hour after hour is spent on a topic that could be reported about in 10 minutes. I surf radio talk shows and hear shock jocks saying how bad whatever the topic of the day is, and how that topic of the day is bringing our country to its knees. And then I remember that most media outlets are no longer committed to the reporting of factual information. They are businesses and businesses exist to make money. To make money, it is necessary to get people's attention and convince them to watch, listen, or read so they can claim market share and charge big dollars for advertising.

Reporting and criticizing public education fits their model well. A high percentage of Americans have kids, grandchildren, or other close relatives in school, and the idea of a "nation at risk" lends itself to fears of disastrous proportions and national security concerns. Remember President Reagan's "shock-jock" introduction to the 1983 study?

> "The educational foundations of our society are presently being eroded by a rising tide of mediocrity that threatens our very future as a Nation and a people…If an unfriendly foreign power had attempted to impose on America the mediocre educational performance that exists today, we might well have viewed it as an act of war."

This is newsworthy! Our nation is at risk! It is a broad generalization that gets people's attention, which can then be used to get them to listen, which in turn gets people to tune in, which then results in more market share and more ad dollars. Few, it seems, take the time to look around, to question the conclusions of the media, having not noticed we no longer live in the days when "reporters" focus on supplying factual "reports" without unsolicited and often amateur editorial overlays. Sadly, the status of journalism as an accountable and honorable profession is tarnished.

As I have maintained from the beginning, public education is not a failure in America, and most of the general public knows it. Yes, it needs improvement, as does any organization or profession, and on an ongoing basis. But creating hysteria to get market share is not only not the solution, but part of the problem that makes real reform impossible.

What has been the result of this political gamesmanship, over-attention to sports, and media sensation-seeking? Erosion of respect for education and the very educators on whose backs these very same legislators, sports writers and commentators, and journalists stood as they climbed to the pinnacle of success.

Decreased Respect for Education and Educators

Ask most in my generation what would have happened when our parents learned that we'd misbehaved at school, and the answer is the same. What the teacher said held much greater weight than our versions of the stories, and for good reason. We respected our teachers because our parents respected our teachers, our community leaders respected our teachers, and our state and federal governments respected our teachers.

As I said in the beginning, as with any other profession, there are and will always be "bad" teachers, but they do not comprise the majority. I can think of no other profession whose members are more important than teachers in the preparation of young minds for the challenges they will face and the opportunities they will be given as adults. And yet, I can also think of no other profession whose members have been more maligned.

Let any one of us have virtually any other problem in an arena about which we know very little, and we seek the advice of professionals in the field—doctors, lawyers, bankers, business and financial advisors, realtors, plumbers. Teachers and other school professionals used to be among them. That is, until about three decades ago, and reports like "A Nation At Risk" appeared on the scene. When the fear-mongering and political manipulation of the public dialogue began to increase, respect and honor for teachers in our society began to erode. So much for public education's goal of sustaining democracy!

Here are some of the reasons I believe the erosion of respect for teachers and the profession itself began.

Written and Unwritten Rules

We are a society of rules. They are a given, providing both protection for all of us and clear guidance for boundaries between us, including the consequences when those rules are violated. Those rules are both written and unwritten.

The written rules are generally straightforward, such as laws of the highway and rules of procedure that must be followed in school, in the workplace, and in general. But the unwritten rules and behaviors must also be learned and practiced in our society to ensure healthy relationships and productivity, and they influence whether or not we interact with each other in a respectful way. Obedience of the written rules and the consequences for failure to obey them are equally straightforward, but in the end, the unwritten rules can have greater impact on a person's success in life.

In school, it is true that most children understand the written rules and expectations for behavior. But if the rules are unwritten, how do we learn what they are? Through the actions of our parents, through stories, through what we see in the media.

If someone is disrespectful to friends, family, co-workers, and supervisors, the results are not pleasant—abandonment, divorce, job termination, prison. And yet…I listen to colleagues and am amazed at how many tell me that while talking with parents, they have been yelled at, challenged, and called names. Trust me, I understand that parents are emotional when talking about their children, but when did such behavior become acceptable in a parent-teacher conference or conversation?

I have been in conferences with parents whose interactions with me were like one of the "reality" shows where "non-actors" yell at each other. Have we reached a point where television defines how we as parents interact with the people who—second only to us—have the greatest influence on our kids?

I hear children tell their friends the negative comments their parents made about teachers at home. I've had students defy simple requests for them to comply with classroom rules, all the while sure that if I call their parents, the parents will defend them without consideration of the misbehavior of their children. I remember calling a parent to report that their child was in a fight and hit another child in the face only to have them tell me "their child would never do that." This, despite the fact that I was the one who saw the fight and broke it up myself.

I don't care if a parent doesn't like me or disagrees with what I say, but I *do* care if the communication of that disagreement undermines my authority in the classroom. Why? Because it renders me even more unable to present the knowledge and skills the child needs to do well. Do you listen to people you don't respect?

With increasing regularity, I see parents giving excuses for why their children have not done projects and homework that other children have completed. Similarly, more and more parents think nothing of taking their children out of school to go on vacation, and yet expect me to accommodate their children by taking extra time to ensure that they make up the work missed. (That's especially irritating when the child tells me they went to Disney World, but the note from their parents say the child was home sick for the week.)

These lessons about respect for teachers and the importance of our roles in their lives, taught by parents, are much more powerful and influential than any lesson an educator can teach in the classroom. And their impact on our enthusiasm is more profound than most imagine.

How did this come to be? I think that, as a society, some measure of parents lost touch with the fact that they, and not teachers, are the number one educators of their children. This was true 50 years ago, and it's true today. Some parents seem to understand this, but increasingly some don't.

As a result of the confluence of politics, sports and media, parents seem to fall loosely into six categories that most teachers recognize:

1. **The Supportive and Involved.** These parents are true partners with us in their child's education. They help their child with school work, support us when we call to inform them their child is not passing a class or got in trouble that day, and they talk about us with their friends and neighbors in a good way. Kids see this relationship and usually respond accordingly, knowing that their teacher(s) and parents are talking to each other and they will not get away with playing us against each other. MOST parents fall into this category.

2. **The Absentee.** We try to get these parents in for conferences, and they confirm but then do not show. We call and leave messages or send email but get no reply. I personally have called parents, only to have them hang up as soon as I introduce myself as their child's teacher. I call back and the phone rings and goes into voice mail.

They do not want to talk with me. It is clear that to help the child of these parents, it is up to me—alone.

3. **The Teacher Bashers.** Although not by any means the majority of parents, these take the biggest toll on the respect that children must have for their teachers in order for us to help them. These parents talk badly about us to their friends in church and at the ball park, and they do it in front of their kids. They proclaim that they're going to move their children to other schools where the teachers are nicer and not so bent on enforcing rules of conduct. Despite their anger and accusations, teachers are expected to slog on. But we're human, too, and the relationship between the No. 1 and No. 2 influences needed to help the child be successful breaks down.

4. **The Blamers.** The children of blaming parents have no responsibility for their academic success. In the minds of these parents, their children are perfect. If they fail a test, a class, or misbehave, it is something the teacher did (or did not) do.

   A student of mine recently failed a test and when I emailed the parents to let them know and to offer a re-take opportunity, their response was, "What did you do to prepare him for the test?" It didn't matter that we'd been talking about the subject in class for two weeks, reviewed every day, and posted a study guide online with the answers.

Another time, I called a parent to let them know their child had started a fight that had caused injury to another child. "Where were *you*?" asked the parent. "My child would never hit anyone." This, despite the fact that I had already said that I'd witnessed the entire incident and stopped the fight, but had not been able to intervene until after the injury had occurred.

5. **The Helicopters.** These parents seem to need to protect their child from "everything." I believe they are well-intentioned, but their behavior is actually at the expense of the social and emotional growth of their children. These parents drive their children to and from school every day because they do not want them to ride on the school bus with "those other children." Their kids aren't allowed to play outside after school because their parents are afraid they might get hurt or kidnapped. They don't want their child to get bad grades, even if they don't understand the material, because "it might hurt their self-esteem."

   Some theorize that since parents are having fewer children nowadays, they are more protective of the one or two they have. In their defense, the impact of societal ills like child pornography, child sex trafficking, kidnapping, sexual abuse, school shootings, drive-by shootings, and bullying, among others, must be overwhelming. Though statistically speaking, there may be only a minute chance that any of these will ever happen to a particular child, the constant barrage on television and the internet is such that our nerves seem to remain on edge.

6. **The Over-achievers.** These parents are a mixture of supportive with the additional component of competition: Their child must be better than everyone else's.

   These parents enroll their children early in piano or violin lessons. They talk about their children getting into the best colleges before they've even reached middle school. They enroll their children in whatever programs or activities they believe to be necessary to get them there.

   I sometimes talk with my students about their week outside of school and get exhausted just listening. They are running, practicing, performing, preparing, and/or doing something every day and evening. Everything is organized, structured, and scheduled. They have very little free time to just relax, involve themselves in free play, or do homework.

   I understand, being one, that parents have for all time wanted their children to grow up and have a life better than theirs. But the costs of defining what "better" means instead of allowing their children to find their own paths will be enormous.

Having said all of that, there's no doubt that the role of parents in public education is critical. No teacher disagrees with the fact that parents must be involved with their child's education or that meaningful dialogue about improving public education must include the parents of the children it serves. In defense of parents today, they are challenged in ways that parents have never been challenged before.

I remind myself daily that Maslow's theory doesn't apply just to children, and the influence of: 1) economic disparity, 2) ethnic and racial discrimination, 3) geographic distance from extended family members, and 4) family dysfunction—ranging from an inability to provide for the basic needs of their children to concerns about their own personal safety—takes its toll on parents as well as children.

- **Sole providers.** Regardless of how they became single parents, one person instead of two is faced with performing all the tasks of parenting—working, doing laundry, running kids to practice, making supper, reading bedtime stories…they are doing the best they can for themselves and their children.
- **Divorced parents.** Friendly or hostile, divorce is hard on children. Many divorces put children in the middle as if they were pawns in a battle. My wife had a student who was out of school because she was called to testify against her father in a custody hearing. I have taught students who left work at one parent's home and—because of their estranged parents' relationship—had no way to retrieve it before it was the first parent's "turn" again.

  We know, too, that the economic circumstances of divorced parents with children—most often their mothers—can be considerably more dire than those of the non-custodial parents. How can we expect parents to be active participants in their child's education when their own lives are being turned upside down?

- **Parents in circumstances of economic hardship.** Lost jobs and the Great Recession have pushed even intact families into bankruptcy, requiring them to lose their homes or sell them in attempts to downsize. Many have been forced to take lower-paying jobs to put food on the table. Unexpected deaths of spouses and high medical bills put extra strain on finances, not to mention the capacities of the surviving parents. The stress of not having enough money for the family and the normal grieving of the loss of a significant other takes precedence over whether the homework is done.
- **"Sandwiched" care-givers.** People today are waiting longer before getting married, which delays the beginning of families. Although often positive in terms of career development and economic stability, this same trend pushes parents of school-aged children on the other end, as more and more are faced with caring for aging parents as well.

We must grapple and solve the negative impacts of social and cultural issues on all of the direct shareholders in public education—students, teachers and parents alike—before we can even begin to address the challenges we face in passing on to children the academic knowledge and skills they will need to thrive in the world they will inherit.

Chapter 8
The Students Themselves

We've talked about the impacts of social issues, political manipulation, the media, and parental attitudes on students and learning in general. But we can't fully address the issues that face public education without discussing the most important direct stakeholders—the children themselves—and how they, themselves, contribute to the system that is public education today.

Where attention is concerned, it is important that we talk about Maslow's hierarchy of needs again. Common sense and experience tell us that when we are hungry, our attention will be focused on food. When we are sleepy or ill, we have problems sustaining attention, even if, unlike young children especially, we know that paying attention to whatever it is important and why. When we are frightened and anxious, whether due to something we've seen or something that we've experienced, our attention is naturally on doing whatever we can to avoid repeating the experience.

No matter how well-prepared and engaging my lesson plans are, an introduction to biology doesn't hold its own against hunger, fatigue, sickness or fear. The reasons that schools offer lunch, medical care, and mental health services for students are not just out of the goodness of our hearts, but in support of the first job of educators: to provide an environment in which learning has the highest odds of taking place.

As the number of children in poverty increases, the number of children who come to school hungry, sick, and sleep-deprived increases as well. Their energies for learning are usurped in favor of fulfilling the simplest of basic biological and physiological needs. What "c-a-t" spells is not high on the list.

As the number of children who are homeless, in foster care, and/or in dysfunctional home situations increases, so too will the number of children who come to school anxious and depressed—their energies for learning sidetracked into seeking a safe haven, not how to convert fractions to decimals.

Children who are neglected and don't get the positive attention they need at home focus on finding ways to get that attention, that love and acceptance. Doing school work or taking standardized tests is not their primary objective. The older they get, the more attractive things like gang membership become and the influence of peer relationships naturally increases. In the classroom, we see it in the form of disruptive students.

There have always been students that are class clowns, students that cannot sit still or be quiet for any length of time, and are sometimes defiant. But where it used to be one or maybe two that were defiant, there are three or more now. The transfer of academic knowledge and skills that is the primary job of teachers takes a back seat to managing the classroom so that the learning of the majority of well-behaved students isn't disturbed.

This is one more way in which larger class sizes wreak havoc. So much energy is expended on managing and dealing with students seeking teachers' attention, whether positive or negative, learning for all decreases. And we're still only at Level 3 with respect to the Maslow pyramid. Before teachers can engage motivation aimed at fulfilling a student's cognitive needs for mastery and achievement, disorders to self-esteem take their tolls.

In the classroom, teachers generally see evidence of two forms of self-esteem: 1) healthy self-esteem, which positively influences self-motivation and achievement, and 2) abnormally deflated or inflated self-esteem, which, like Level 1 - 3 needs, take attention away from academic tasks.

Children with healthy self-esteem begin to differentiate between their importance and acceptability as people and their unique strengths and weaknesses. They do not feel diminished when they don't know something and don't overestimate their value when they do and others don't. "Success" and "failure" in school are circumstances that signal that they have achieved mastery of a subject or haven't quite *yet*. They work with parents and teachers to develop strategies for learning the things they don't yet know—more review, previewing, fewer activities, whatever it takes.

Learned helplessness

Back in the late 1960s, as a psychology graduate student, Martin Seligman did an experiment in which dogs were placed in one side of two-sided cages where they experienced a series of light shocks. In one cage, the door between the "shock" side and the "no-shock" sides was open. In the other, the door was closed.

Dogs in both "door open" and "door closed" cages initially scrambled around, looking for ways out of the condition, and eventually, the dogs in the "door open" situation learned to jump through to the other side to avoid the shock. Dogs in the "door closed" situation, however, eventually gave up trying and just lay down.

But that wasn't the most shocking result, pardon the pun. It was when Seligman opened the doors of the cages of the dogs previously denied access to the "no-shock" side of the cage before.

What happened? *Absolutely nothing.* They had "learned" that they were "helpless," *that they had no power* to change what had happened to them. Although the solution to the problem was right there in front of them, the dogs no longer sought a way out.

When faced with a repeated label of failure, children with low self-esteem often give up trying in school. For them, they have not failed. They *are* failures, and the difference in impact to achievement is devastating. Without the experience of early academic success, which is the best motivator for learning and achievement, they're forced to "defend" against the idea that they are not as smart as other students. To avoid the feeling, when they are confused or don't understand something, they check out.

It's less painful to make an "F" for not turning in homework than to let into consciousness the albeit incorrect conclusion that they're not liked or considered as important or valuable as other kids who know the answers.

Another form of entitlement

On the other end of that spectrum, the children with artificially *inflated* self-esteem are equally handicapped, because their self-esteem is tied to the fact that they're "smart" or "talented" and the belief that it's a fixed and immutable fact. These children don't make the connection between effort and academic achievement. They often develop a sense of entitlement and depend on extrinsic rewards for motivation.

These are the children who grew up receiving praise and trophies for participating, no matter the quality of their participation. Many of these students expect teachers to give them good grades, study guides to memorize for the tests, and some reward for doing anything above or beyond minimal expectations in the class. I have actually been asked by some students what I was going to "give" them in order for them to do additional work on a research paper or simply asked them to help clean up after an activity. They are the students that argue, pout, or believe they deserve a better grade when they do not earn an "A" on a project or assignment.

About the time they get to me, in middle school, they begin to confront the reality that the reason they're in school at all is that there is something they don't know that we can teach them. Kids who have never faced dealing with the inevitable failures in life suffer blows to self-esteem that result in declining performance at school.

Apathy, or Failure to Connect School to Their Lives

Somewhere in the middle are children for whom school seems irrelevant. They don't necessarily misbehave, but don't see the connection between school and the reality of their everyday lives. This may relate to an earlier discussion of the fact that we have drifted toward preparing students for entry into traditional college environments, a goal many students do not have. Their parents did not attend college or university and have done quite well, or no one in their extended family has ever gone to college and there are no expectations for them to go either.

This again points to our need to reexamine and agree on the purpose public education should fulfill. If it is to address preparing ALL students for tomorrow's workplace, I think we need initiatives that support not only preparation for "higher education," but apprenticeships and vocational education, as in the past.

Having said that, however, the purpose of this book is not to delve into specifics of curriculum but to lay out general factors that must be considered in developing an all-encompassing plan for reforming education.

Learning Disabilities

In an earlier chapter, we discussed the fact that the act of learning is a neurological event, which means that when it takes place, it isn't an action done *to* us, nor is it something that takes place in a *group* of people. It takes place (or doesn't) in the brains of individual students.

To take the point further, because no politician, school board, principal, teacher, or parent can directly change what happens in another person's brain, education is an indirect process of communication, involving both student and teacher.

If you've ever tried to communicate to your spouse or significant other that you've been invited to a party on Tuesday night while s/he is busy watching something on television, you know what I mean. Tuesday rolls around and it is as if the conversation never occurred. Likewise, for communication that results in learning to occur, a student's attention must be focused on the knowledge or skill at hand, and his or her attention sustained long enough for the information to be transferred from short-term to long-term memory. By default, anything that interferes with attention and memory interferes with the "normal" learning process.

We have talked about the needs that must be fulfilled in order for humans of all ages to maximize their own personal potentials and reach their own definitions of success. We've discussed the political, social, and cultural influences that support and interfere with the fulfillment of those needs. What's remains is a fundamental issue that directly impacts individual students and the process of learning itself, and indirectly affects high-stakes test scores more than any other single factor—learning disabilities, including Attention Deficit Disorder.

It should go without saying that if attention is key to learning, ADD/ADHD significantly affects it. As of 2014, about 6.4 million children have received an ADHD diagnosis at some point. That number has increased 16% since 2007 and *53% in the past decade.*

In general, what we call "learning disabilities" are relatively persistent brain-related dysfunctions that most often affect the *speed* with which new learning takes place. This is especially important to know with respect to the development of foundational skills—the ability to read, the ability to understand and apply numerical concepts, the ability to process what is heard and make sense of it, the ability to express verbally and on paper what one understands, among others. To quote from a 2014 report from the National Center for Learning Disabilities:

> Learning disabilities are not caused by visual, hearing or motor disabilities, intellectual disabilities (formerly referred to as mental retardation), emotional disturbance, cultural factors, limited English proficiency, environmental or economic disadvantages, or inadequate instruction. However, there is a higher reported incidence of learning disabilities among people living in poverty, perhaps due to increased risk of exposure to poor nutrition, ingested and environmental toxins (e.g., lead, tobacco and alcohol) and other risk factors during early and critical stages of development. (p. 3)

Let me hasten to say that learning disabilities are *not* a death sentence. Because a child has a learning disability doesn't mean that he or she cannot learn to read or perform calculations. Untold numbers of adults who have struggled all of their lives with reading and other skills are likely to have some form of undiagnosed learning disability. Fortunately, our brains are remarkable, and even when certain areas of the brain don't act as they do for the majority of people, alternative areas sometimes take up the slack.

However, as going around a washed-out bridge to get to a destination means that it will take you longer to get there, so does discovering and applying methods for compensating for necessary skills for learning-disabled students. It is a fact of life—they require *more time and more practice* to develop the strategies for reading, doing math calculations, and writing they will use for the rest of their lives.

As many learning disabilities seem linked to genetics—the odds that one of a dyslexic child's parents is also dyslexic, for example, are relatively high—*there is nothing a student or teacher can actively do to speed up the process.* When we consider the fact that 100% of high-stakes tests are "power" tests, meaning the scores are based not only on what a student knows but how many questions he can answer within an allotted amount of time, are they an accurate assessment of what students know? Is it more important that a child know how to read fast or that he reads at all?

All other things aside, students themselves—through no fault of their own—present obstacles to the learning process. Although many fall into my categories of "natural learners" and "goal-oriented learners," by all indications, the number of students whose basic biological and physiological needs are not fulfilled are increasing. The number of students diagnosed with some form of learning disability is rising, correlated with increasing numbers living in conditions of poverty, poor nutrition and medical care, and neglect. The number of students who are transient, have become apathetic, are disruptive in class…is increasing.

On top of that, more students than ever either feel a sense of entitlement, exhibited by expectations of do-overs and free passes for failure to do assigned work or prepare for tests. Still others suffer from deflated self-esteem due to learned helplessness.

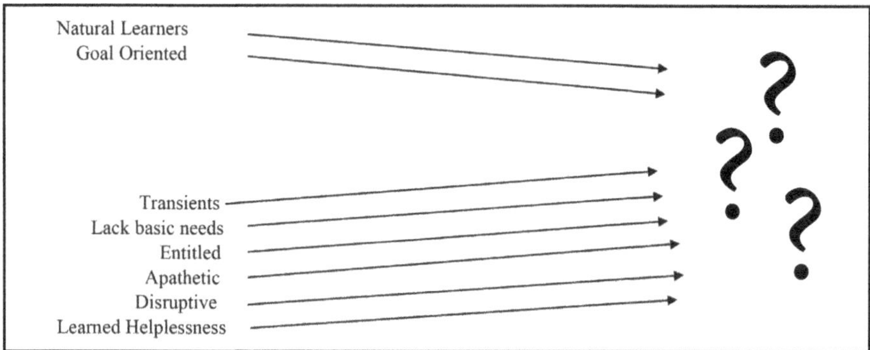

Most teachers can engage the natural and goal-oriented learners. Visit any mainstream class in a college of education, and the skills and pedagogy taught there are based on the assumption that the majority of children a new teacher will encounter fall into these categories. But increasingly, the challenges presented by ever-rising numbers of children who fall into the other categories make that assumption a moot point.

What will be the result if the miasma of culture, social pressures and economic hardship continues? Where will we be without a comprehensive strategic plan—based in reality and focused on solutions that involve all facets of our society? If they haven't already been, the capacities of even veteran teachers will be stretched to the breaking point.

Teachers can only do so much.

Chapter 9
The Teachers

If I want to improve the gas mileage of my car, I can inflate my tires to the proper air pressure and maybe get a mile extra per gallon. I can drive 55 m.p.h. instead of 70 on the highway. I can accelerate slowly from stop lights instead of focusing on how fast I can get from zero to 50. These are small individual changes that I can make to get maybe a couple miles per gallon more.

But if I want *major* improvements in gas mileage, bringing about the changes by myself is beyond my capabilities. The designers need to make my car lighter and less wind-resistant. They need to redesign my car's fuel-injection system and recalibrate its transmission to create a better energy transfer ratio between the engine and drive wheels. Manufacturers need to redesign tires to be more energy efficient while keeping the cost of production down, and petroleum refineries must be charged with creating a more efficiently burning fuel.

Public education is like my car, and substantial improvements to it require that we look at the bigger picture. If all the changes suggested by policymakers are aimed at the teacher without regard to all of the other contributing factors, only small and irregular improvements will be gained.

Like all of the other variables affecting students today, there is no question that the training, personalities, and competence of teachers impact public education. But until we simultaneously consider all the facets of the system—social factors, health factors, and economic factors affecting students, parents, and teachers, we will achieve little toward reforming the lifeblood of our leadership in the world. Until teachers are free to focus on making their classrooms conducive for learning and work in situations where there is ample time to devote to knowing their individual students, their learning styles, their challenges, we will be unable to fulfill the missions we set out to accomplish when we aspired to teach.

In my 20+ years of teaching, I have met teachers of many stripes—different personalities, different energy levels, different styles of teaching. I have met teachers of various levels of competence in their subject areas and methods, and a wide range of experiences, from urban to rural schools, from affluent areas and high-risk situations. I hear teachers talk about what the media, the legislators, parents, kids, business leaders, and others are saying to them directly and indirectly.

There is a commonality in the type of people who decide to enter the teaching profession and stay—they live to see the light go on in their students' eyes, whether a kindergartner who learns the word "hat" or the civics student who sees the checks and balances of our executive, legislative and judiciary branches of government. But I also hear something else—fatigue, frustration, discouragement. We are trained, capable human beings, but because we are not superhuman, we are limited in our ability to overcome many of the obstacles our students face.

Media and Teachers

Teachers are in the news a lot. Newspapers, television, talk shows, and the internet seem to cover teacher stories more than those of any other single profession.

There are good and bad sides to this fascination/coverage. There's no doubt that a teacher stealing money from a school should go to jail and make amends. There's no doubt that teachers who change student test answers for a financial bonus should go to jail. There's no doubt that teachers who become intimately involved with students should be prosecuted.

I suppose our society's fascination with misery brings media the ratings they seek, but there are thousands of stories about successes, good things that are happening in our schools other than the winning of state championships in football or other sports—students winning STEM competitions, mock trial competitions, one-act play competitions, and teachers named "the best of the best" by their students.

Teacher Evaluation

Teacher evaluation systems have been in the news a lot also, once again touted as a way to improve teachers and, therefore, public education in America.

I don't take issue with the suggestion that teacher evaluation systems need to be redone—I agree that they do. But I *do* take issue with the fact that politicians apparently think they have the ability and authority to decide what the criteria for teaching proficiency are.

I understand that, as government employees, we are public servants, but I don't see exams for firefighters, garbage collectors, tax revenue officials, or the legislators themselves in the news, nor do I see "reform packages" designed by anyone outside of those professions. I don't see the job descriptions and performance review criteria of corporate CEOs or any other professions publicly debated, except, perhaps, the training of police officers, due to the recent up-tick of stories from Ferguson to Baltimore and more. Nobody outside Apple has yet had the arrogance to suggest how the company should approach the job performance of their engineers even though millions own iPhones. Few would suggest that they have the experience or expertise to do such a thing, but the same logic doesn't apply to teachers. Apparently, just having attended school once upon a time makes you a master teacher.

As with any other occupation, the measurements of teacher proficiency must be demonstrated to have relevance to performance of the job itself, and those tasked with evaluation must be experts in the evaluation process. No matter where you go, teacher proficiency measures are based on the same things, and rightly so. To be an excellent teacher, you need to know your subject area or areas. You need to provide a physically and emotionally safe environment for your students. You need to know your students—understanding what their unique challenges are and what they're capable of learning. You need to understand how humans learn and how to present material in such a way that your students have the greatest opportunity to get it. You need to stay abreast of new research, both in your content area and in teaching methods.

Of course, some measure of student progress should figure into the equation since the desired outcome is student learning, but *not if that measure can't be shown to correlate to the outcomes desired in the first place.* There is conflicting evidence to suggest that scores on high-stakes tests predict future student success—as I write this, the "new" SAT has been rolled out in response to the fact that many colleges and universities were abandoning SAT scores as admissions criteria because the "old" SAT had proven to be a poor predictor of who would succeed and who wouldn't.

As I suggested early on, if we must use quantitative measures in service to the "numbers god"—and to some degree, we must—the comparisons we make must be made between apples and apples. If you want to measure my proficiency based on student scores, make sure you compare the test scores of my students to the test scores of students of other 7th grade science teachers, students of similar societal influences and socio-economic status. Compare them to students in schools in suburban areas like mine. Make sure that the number of students receiving Title I services in the school I'm compared to is similar to that in my school. If 65 percent of my students are receiving free/reduced lunches, make sure that the percentage of students receiving free/reduced in the other schools is statistically close. If we're going to compare the scores of my students with those in Finland...you get the point.

A retired high school English teacher I know was especially gifted in teaching remedial English to ninth-grade kids who had failed in other attempts. She was once asked if she thought she would ever be chosen as a STAR teacher. "Not likely," she said, "because few of the kids I teach will even take the SAT." Given that STAR Teachers are chosen by STAR students, who are by definition those who score highest on the SAT, were her skills as a teacher considered less than those of a teacher in advanced placement or gifted classrooms? Yes, according to some. But I would maintain that the teacher who could engage and excite students who had failed over and over was far more skilled. Once again, student scores on a high-stakes standardized test are often the criteria for teacher excellence, yet a teacher whose students achieved against the odds would seldom be in the running for such an honor.

"Those who can't, teach."

I was watching a movie recently where a student was arrested and accused of killing someone. The next scene showed her with one of her teachers, whom she had called instead of her attorney. The student obviously trusted the teacher, most likely because the teacher had positively impacted the student's life. In the middle of the scene, the student's attorney burst into the room yelling for the teacher to go away and not talk to his client. "Those who can, DO," he yelled. "Those who can't, TEACH!"

It wasn't the first time I'd heard this epithet, and it probably won't be the last. And in some professions, I suppose it could be true—especially in higher education, where the primary focus is information and students are held responsible for the majority of their learning. But not in Pre-K-12 classrooms.

I'm a middle school teacher of students in grades 6–8, but I wasn't always. My passion has always been about the outdoors so I attended college in the 70s with the goal of working in environmental protection. I was fortunate—when I graduated, I was able to work for the federal government in environmental protection for seven years. After my wife and I got married, my wife was transferred and I followed. I tried to stay in civil service but it didn't work out. At that point, I became employee number 13 of a small computer software startup. After six years, during which I, as sales manager, contributed to the growth from $1 million to $10 million in sales, I was ready for a change again. My wife asked, "Now what do you want to do?" and I replied, "Become a teacher." And I did.

When I worked in the civil service, and in corporate world, I was treated as a professional. I had a business card, went on business lunches, and closed deals. No one in the media, no politicians called me a failure. Before becoming a teacher, I went to the bathroom when I needed to. I had an hour for lunch and if it took a little longer, it was not a problem—I was a professional and everyone understood I would make up the time.

Since becoming a teacher, I pee in the boy's bathroom with my students on the way back from lunch, which is 25 minutes—including the walk to and from. I eat at the teacher's table with 12 adults surrounded by 300 13-year-olds. Since becoming a teacher, I have had elected officials mandate programs to make me a "better teacher." I have had district offices tell me what canned reform package to use because it worked in Texas. (I am in Georgia.)

Over and over, I've heard critics of public education make comments like, "Only those that cannot make it in engineering, accounting, (insert virtually anything here) become teachers." I have heard people say that teachers choose the profession so they can have summers off. More times than I care to count, I've heard people I know have never stood in front of a classroom of students aged 4 to 18, say, "How hard can it be?"

As one who came to teaching late, who succeeded in the public sector and the corporate world, I can say without reservation that if you chose to teach because you couldn't make it in other jobs or just wanted a "cushy" job with summers off, you're either miserable or no longer teaching.

In the early 2000s, when there was a teacher shortage, I met several people who wanted to become teachers through "alternative certification" methods. They were professionals from the sciences, the military, and the corporate arena who wanted to become teachers after working in their fields—all without going through a college teacher preparation program. In my state, they had four weeks of training over the summer, then started the school year, agreeing to attend evening and weekend classes throughout the year.

I remember talking to one woman who was a biologist and wanted to teach children science. As we prepared for the first day of school, she tried to impress me and our fellow teachers by telling us how much biology she knew and how the kids were going to learn from her. I sensed none of the passion nor an understanding of children as we talked. In retrospect, I guess she thought the kids would be in awe of her expertise, but after five days of pre-planning and just three days of kids in the classroom, she walked out and never returned.

Kids know when teachers know their stuff but they also know when they care about them, want to know them, and love them. I confess that I never loved any of the people I sold computer services to, but I can honestly say that I love my "customers" now.

It has now been two decades since I became a teacher. I look back with few regrets. Although I took a significant pay cut when I became a teacher, I realized that there is more to life than just making money. It took me until my late thirties, with a lovely wife, three daughters, and a job I did not enjoy, to choose the profession I am called to. In some ways, I am jealous of those who chose to become teachers out of high school because they figured it out much earlier than me.

Teachers choose teaching because they have a calling to make a difference in the lives of children. Inherent in them is an altruistic need to help others that is not driven by money or status unless the money they make isn't enough for them to survive. Constantly demeaned and criticized by elected officials, by the media and often the general public, they keep coming to school every morning and working late into the night grading papers, sometimes at the expense of their own family lives.

In order to be successful, a teacher must have an understanding of how we learn and what healthy development involves—and patience like no other profession.

An assistant principal once told my wife that teachers must be able to forgive. His point was that there are days a child will drive you crazy and make you angrier than ever before. But the next day when that child comes through the doors, there can be no grudges and no revenge, no attempts to get the child "fired," as in the workplace.

Because we know we are second only to parents in influencing our students' success, we know that one part of the job is to do the best to help a child grow up, to meet the non-academic challenges of the world they will inhabit with the skills to navigate those challenges as well.

Teaching is part art, part science. Where there are certain parts of the profession that can be indirectly measured, it cannot be reduced to a cookbook approach. The approaches of science, as in life sciences, cannot be applied here. Why? As I've said over and over, kids are not widgets that can be processed, poured knowledge into, and expected to come off the assembly line 12 years later, smarter and ready to go to college or work.

Teaching is an art. Yes, we need to learn the general mechanics, fundamentals, and skills required to help children learn, but every child and classroom is different. So is every teacher. There are no formulas or models or "best ways" to teach that apply to all students.

Teachers must take everything they have learned and apply it in their own unique situations, unique classrooms, unique schools, unique parent interactions, and unique local communities. Our masterpieces are our students—some we paint with oils, some water, some acrylics.

You do not become a teacher because you could not succeed in any other profession. You become a teacher because you love children. Take it from me as one who has did something else first. Those who CAN, teach.

The messages teachers (and everyone else) are hearing

The absence of a single, coherent definition for public school success and the inability to establish guidelines for how to measure progress and achievement because of that absence, continue to contribute to the frustration and rhetoric surrounding teachers. As long as scoring number one in the world on high-stakes exams is tops on the nation's priority list, no substantive reform can happen. At every level of government, scoring high on some mandated exam is accepted as the definition of success. School scores and rankings, tied to funding formulas, are based on test results. Teacher evaluations are based in varying degrees on test results. Decisions about whether students are promoted to the next grade are made based on test results. Student placement in gifted and resource classes is based on test results.

It's pretty clear—the message teachers (and the public) have received in the past few years is that the "successful performance" of their jobs will be defined, NOT by the number of students who understand the subjects they are teaching and can apply the skills they learned, but by how many students get high scores on one-time multiple-choice standardized test administrations.

If we apply the principles of teaching, treating tests for what they are, with all their limitations, children with a true education will do well on the tests anyway. They did before 1983, when funding formulas and definitions of "failing" schools were first tied to the tests. Yes, there was an income-achievement gap that needed attention. But the path we would travel to remedy that was one that would prove to be ineffective, and the fault would be laid at the feet of teachers.

We jumped the track when politicians, who knew little or nothing about the process of education, took over the reins, and began to employ the equally uninformed media to change the public perception to support their political agendas.

Then, as now, there were many who predicted what was about to happen—that when money to operate schools, including the number of teachers and the salaries of those tasked with ensuring that students learn what they need to know academically—were tied to test scores, things would change, but not for the better. Why not? Because test scores were not and are not a sufficient criterion of school success.

But, when so much is at stake, the focus in the classroom turns to the criterion used to measure success, whether that measure is relevant or not. What happened in the Atlanta Public Schools, where teachers were apparently asked by their supervisors to change test score answers, was clearly wrong, but it isn't surprising. The pressure to attend to test performance over meeting the needs of children with varied needs is understandable. But its result has been a systemic failure to support teachers in making their classrooms as *conducive to learning* as possible for the unique population of students assigned there in any given semester or school year.

Within the walls of my classroom, inspite of the real challenges of different learning styles and known learning disabilities brought to me by the students themselves, I can control the physical and emotional safety of my students, minimize disruptions (if supported by school administrators and parents), and devise and execute lesson plans that engage students and deliver knowledge to them about life science topics. That is the job I signed on for. Those are the responsibilities for which I should be held accountable.

But my peers and I are not superhuman. I cannot ensure that the children who come into my classroom malnourished benefit from the lessons I prepare. I cannot ensure that they get eight hours of sleep the night before. I cannot stop the emotional effects of divorce, abuse, economic hardship, homelessness, or the death of a parent.

The influences affecting school success are much stronger than the effects of teachers alone. I have had more than one parent admit to my colleagues and me that she didn't know what to do with her child and was hoping I could "fix" him or her.

But the messages we hear suggest that the public, media, politicians, business leaders, and parents are asking teachers to somehow repair the children where other teachers have failed, inspiring them to be self-motivated and somehow changing the neurons in their brains. Among other things, it's our fault that kids are not:

- succeeding in school
- graduating from high school
- passing their classes
- measuring up to students in other countries
- going on to college
- overcoming the social obstacles they face
- overcoming learning disabilities, ADHD, and other brain-related issues

After one of the school shooting tragedies, I even heard a media talking head suggest that it was the *teachers'* faults because they did not recognize and identify the teenage gunman as a threat to others and his classmates. Sorry, but attending a law enforcement academy or diagnosis of mental illness was not a course in my education curriculum—nor should it have been.

As a society, since 1983 and "The Nation at Risk" study, we have publicly fought over who's to blame for the imagined sins and ills of public education and the outcome has been *the collective targeting of teachers.* Failing to hold ourselves accountable as a nation, we have contributed to the problems in our schools by allowing politicians on both sides of the aisle to make public education a subject of campaign rhetoric.

We have created an educational culture in which common sense no longer prevails, in which how and why we humans learn and don't is ignored. Instead, students, teachers, and school districts are rewarded or punished based on numbers on statistical graphs. We say that we want what is best for the students, comparing them to other countries, but the support networks for our children bear no resemblance to what other countries have in place, and the standards cannot be points on a graph if we expect to accomplish that goal.

Teachers are human. As I said in the section on class sizes, I will focus the curriculum I teach to maximize progress toward the established goal of high-stakes test scores if it directly impacts my ability to provide for my family, just as I did when I worked for a company with sales quotas and plans to achieve them. We all may continue down that path to our collective demise, but I do not believe we will, because in my heart, I do not believe that is what America wants.

What Do Teachers Want?

So what do teachers want? Show us respect as the professionals we are. Trust us to do our jobs. Change standards and curricula when necessary, but implement them realistically over time, and then leave them alone. Quit changing the rules in midstream, and don't tie our livelihoods to achievement of standards irrelevant to the goals you demand. Acknowledge that we are only a part of the problem of public education. As citizens, parents, administrators, businesspeople, and elected officials, take responsibility for your contributions to the social and economic issues that make it impossible for us to do our jobs. Work with us, not against us, laying all of the blame at our feet.

Treat us as the professionals we are.

The alternative certification programs of the early 2000s are fine examples of the lack of respect certain legislators and the general public have for the teaching profession, suggesting that becoming a teacher requires little more than a low-level training course for orderlies in a hospital environment. But it requires considerably more.

As with virtually every other professional degree—from pre-med to business administration—teachers earn four-year-degrees, studying everything from human cognitive development to theories of learning to methodologies for interacting with children in ways that have a high probability of motivating and engaging them. Despite the slurs we often hear, there are no courses for "Advanced Bulletin Board Design." Continuing education requirements for maintaining licensure are similar to those for doctors and lawyers, as are graduate programs conferring master's degrees and doctorates.

Include us in any conversations that impact students and their learning. Include us on boards, committees, and legislative councils that develop policies, rules, and standards that it will fall to us to implement. We are the experts on how to best educate our children, the experts on what is actually happening every day in our schools, the experts on what will, might, and *won't* improve the issues that confront us.

Trust us to do our jobs.

Put the word "micromanage" in an online search, and you will find article after article about how to avoid micro-managing your employees or how to "manage a micro-managing boss." The complaints come from every industry, from the military complex to doctors in hospitals to sales teams. The term describes people in authority over others who dictate not only the outcomes and responsibilities of the jobholder's position, but attempt to control in micro-terms how a job will be performed, with no apparent awareness that different people work in different ways and often in more efficient and effective ways than the manager herself. Even worse is the manager who never did the job and has no training or expertise in conducting personnel evaluations. In most cases, these managers directly impact whether those who report to them are rewarded with raises and evaluated for promotions.

Micromanagement from outside is not epidemic in the business arena, but for teachers, the reality is sometimes quite the opposite. From head teachers to administrators who taught only a few years in the classroom to governmental authorities who have not been in a classroom since they graduated from high school to parents whose children could not possibly have a problem, we are forced to comply with micromanagement from all sides, but we dare not complain if we want to keep our jobs.

We are trained professionals and have chosen the teaching profession because we want to be with the children, helping them learn and grow up. We all know that new teachers especially need some measure of mentoring—one session of student teaching is not enough to acquaint new teachers with the challenges they may face. But mentoring isn't micromanagement, and the mentoring must be done by people who've been in their shoes.

It is human nature that when we are trusted by others to do our jobs without constant criticism or time-wasting mandates that solve problems that do not exist, we rise and accomplish great things. But when pushed, pulled, and beaten down, even the most talented of employees eventually go through the motions, or leave and seek other jobs. In some states, good teachers are running for the doors. And despite the assumptions of many, it usually isn't about money.

Maintain stability with respect to performance standards.

We understand that the world is changing and the knowledge required to function in today's world is exponentially greater than it was when we were in school. We recognize the need for new, more aggressive standards. But we also recognize that the implementation of new standards cannot be performed overnight.

At intervals, new standards are set at state or district levels, followed by changes in curriculum developed by district professionals, which is then sent to teachers. New standards don't negate the need to deliver the same information we've been teaching—they usually just increase the number of things we must fit into a fixed period of time. As long as school years continue to last for 180 days, there will naturally be an adjustment period every time a new set of performance standards is introduced.

It's no different from being assigned additional responsibility in the corporate workplace, except that there, adults are required to adjust *only their routines.* If as a sales professional I was asked to increase the number of sales calls I made, I had to rethink the way I structured my weeks, which calls I might have made onsite before could be made by phone, and make other logistical changes. I was the only one affected.

Teachers have another step. We have to read, absorb, process, and internalize the new standards and curriculum, get training on new subjects or recommended methods or train ourselves (with reduced budgets, training is often the first thing to go), and *then* adjust that curriculum to fit the specific groups of children we work with—based on their learning abilities and the climate in the school.

Even parents must be fully apprised of what to expect—especially if their childrens' scores on tests may at first go down, as we would expect if information they have not yet been exposed to is included. We must assure parents that the scores will not adversely affect their children, and then make sure they don't.

Above all, allow enough time for the full implementation of new standards to take place before labeling schools, teachers and students as "failing" or comparing them to other schools, other states, and certainly other nations. To establish new policies aimed at correcting problems that are only artifacts of the process of change itself is not only ill-advised, but counterproductive, especially when done as a political response to legislators, the media, and parents who are not faced with managing the changes they mandate.

Make sure that student achievement scores quoted compare apples to apples.

If you're going to use student test scores to evaluate our performance, make sure that you don't penalize us for things over which we have no control. Don't insult our intelligence or yours by suggesting that the reason the students of a teacher of learning-disabled children or a remedial urban high school English class haven't achieved on the same level of those in a gifted class is a lack of proficiency on our parts.

Acknowledge what we are responsible for and what we're not.

I'm not talking about awards, pats on the back or gold stars. I'm talking about acknowledgment that teachers are not solely responsible for the state of public education today. If you take away only one thing from this book, let it be that if public education is failing (and I still say it isn't), teachers are not the sole or primary culprits. And whatever changes and reforms must be made, teachers must be included at every phase. The issues are many and the interrelation of them too complex to ignore the input of the people who spend more time with students than anyone else.

In closing, I hope you see that we are not asking for anything more than those of any other profession. There are management books and management seminars and management systems ad nauseum, all pointing to the idea that to get the most productivity out of employees, they must be respected and treated as the capable professionals they are. Tell them what needs to be done, clearly define the outcomes sought, give them the resources they need to accomplish them, and then leave them mostly alone to perform the job.

Micro-management, especially by those who have barely fulfilled or never held the roles they are placed in authority over, fosters an atmosphere where the jobholders do not feel trusted, and eventually don't make the extra effort to go beyond the call of duty for fear of reprisal. Constant feedback about how lousy a job they are doing pulls employee morale down to levels most organizations cannot build back up for years, if at all.

With teachers, it is no different. The negativity of toxic judgments, blame, and disrespect from the media, politicians, and parents has taken its toll. Labeling us all as "failing," "incompetent," "in it for ourselves" further undermines the enthusiasm of all teachers.

The source doesn't matter—the effect has been toxic. Show us the respect we deserve. Tell us what you want, provide us with the tools we need, and leave us to do what we know is necessary to achieve great things with the children. We know they are the future of our nation and we accept the responsibility.

Trust us – we will do what needs to be done.

Chapter 10
The Edu-System
A Holistic Approach for looking at Public Education

Public education in America is complex. It is a system of people, organizations, special interests, ideas, ideals, and hopes for the future. And it's critical for the future of our country. Education can lift someone from the throngs of poverty and depression to great heights. It can also impact people in negative, unintended ways that some people never overcome. It is political and personal.

In order to improve public education in America, open and honest conversations must occur. One's ideals and beliefs are important but those of others are too. For productive conversations to occur, people must be honest, rational, understanding, and truly want what is best for all and our country, not focus on what is best for themselves or exclusive groups to which they belong. When we look at all the influences of society and their impact on schools, there will be no easy solutions, but they all must be considered if we are to achieve the mission.

Variables of Societal Influence

As we've discussed throughout this book, the influence of societal factors on children and teachers must be an integral part of any conversation about improving our system of education. There has been much discussion in recent years about the effect of poverty on a child's ability to learn, but it is not the only variable and the obvious (and not-so-obvious) effects are not the only ones. It is not one factor that makes a difference for all children—it is a multitude of them, each of which have their enmeshed impacts (positive and negative) on a child.

Our schools are like food webs or chains. Every organism in the food web is important in its own way to the ultimate health of all organisms in the web. Some relationships we may not easily recognize but when something interferes with the web, the health of the entire system becomes threatened.

That is where public education is today. Too many pieces of the whole have changed in such a way that the system as a whole is threatened. We must look at the issue holistically and honestly to create solutions.

The list that follows is not complete, but it is a beginning. As we begin to look at public education and an edu-system of interacting influences, we will see more things that must be addressed. Some influences will have more of an impact in certain regions of the country than others. There will be cases where one factor may impact a child in a severely negative way in one region but not in another because of more effective interventions. So, when we begin to have these conversations, they must start on a local level, taking into account all of the unique pressures and the cumulative impact of all positive and negative influences present at that location at that time.

What if we rated each child, parent, community, school, and teacher based on the same scales, relating to conditions in which they all operate and then put them all together for comparison's sake? For instance, if we looked at each of the categories: Student Basic Needs, Parental Situation, Community Environment, Classroom Environment and the Attitudes/Perspectives of the students themselves, and used a 5-point Likert scale to rate subcategories under each, what crucial information that we're currently missing would be revealed? Doesn't it make sense that we look at the interactions of all the factors in play in order to form a strategic plan that has a chance of addressing the actual obstacles we face?

1 2 3 4 5

STUDENT BASIC NEEDS (MASLOW)		
NEGATIVE INFLUENCE	<—EFFECT ON LEARNING—>	**POSITIVE INFLUENCE**
Hungry every day		Hunger not an issue
Minimal love at home		Loving home life
Abusive home (verbal, physical, sexual)		No known abuse
Neglected		Parents fulfill basic needs
Unstable living arrangements		Same home for many years
At or below poverty level		Money not a concern

1 2 3 4 5

STUDENT PARENTAL SITUATIONS		
NEGATIVE INFLUENCE	<—EFFECT ON LEARNING—>	**POSITIVE INFLUENCE**
One parent/adult in household No extended family support		Two-parent family intact, Extended family support
Hostile parent-child relationship		Healthy parent-child relationship
Parent(s) dropped out of high school		Parent(s) completed post-secondary work
Parent(s) work multiple jobs to provide for basic needs		Parent(s) have comfortable incomes and are home every evening

1 2 3 4 5

COMMUNITY/NEIGHBORHOOD

NEGATIVE INFLUENCE	<—EFFECT ON LEARNING—>	POSITIVE INFLUENCE
High crime rate		Low or no crime
No community involvement in education-related activities		Active parent-teacher organizations, community booster clubs for sports, bands

1 2 3 4 5

SCHOOL/CLASSROOM/TEACHING POLICIES/ENVIRONMENT

NEGATIVE INFLUENCE	<—EFFECT ON LEARNING—>	POSITIVE INFLUENCE
Class sizes, 30+ students		Small class sizes - <25 students
Low parental involvement		High, appropriate parental involvement
Redos on homework, tests expected		No retakes of tests expected
Punitive atmosphere for teachers		Supportive atmosphere for teachers
Parents hostile, absent, unsupportive		Parents active, communicative
School board dysfunctional; mandates policies without input from teachers		School board productive, policies defined with input from teachers, administrators, community leaders, parents
Goals and objectives unclear, policies constantly changing, measurements of student and teacher performance disconnected from stated desired outcomes		Goals and objectives clearly defined, curriculum stable and teachers/students informed well in advance, clear connection between outcomes and measurement

1 2 3 4 5

CHILDREN/STUDENTS

NEGATIVE INFLUENCE	<—EFFECT ON LEARNING—>	POSITIVE INFLUENCE
Sense of entitlement		Focus on effort, reward
Apathetic about schoolwork		Engaged in schoolwork
Too many activities outside of school, including working		Reasonable balance between school, extra-curricular activities
Externally motivated		Intrinsically motivated
Heroes are athletes, movie stars, entertainers		Heroes are scientists, engineers, writers
Need constant attention		Not constantly seeking attention
Tied to technology		Able to entertain self without technology
Un-/Misdiagnosed learning disabilities		Resources aligned with student abilities

These are just a sampling of some of the issues we could start with. Moving forward requires that we consider, at a minimum, all of the variables above and many more of which I am unaware—and how they all influence—positively and negatively—the achievement of the outcomes we are looking for.

My intent here is to show how complex the interrelationship of factors affecting public education truly are and how we cannot focus only on one area and expect to achieve the results we want. We MUST consider all the known factors to determine the real cause and effect relationships between the variables themselves and stop assigning blame on the basis of issues that have little or no demonstrated bearing at all.

If teachers who have historically taken their students to high levels and have been rated as highly proficient, find themselves in schools 1) where the poverty level is high, 2) where many of the kids have a single mom working more than one job, 3) in a crime-ridden neighborhood, where teachers don't feel trusted to carry out their responsibilities in a proficient manner, and 4) where a majority of children come to school hungry, relying on the school for most of their meals, what happens to the teacher ratings?

In the current view, the same teacher will be rated now as a low-quality teacher. However, no matter how many times you change out the spark plugs in the car I described in the beginning of Chapter 9, if the actual problem is an undiagnosed oil leak, *the car will continue to break down.*

A teacher in a state near the one I teach in retired from teaching in a high school known for its high achievement scores, and was called back to teach at another high school in her city, one whose achievement scores were consistently lower than the first. All was well until a meeting was called to discuss a new program where teachers from her original high school would be paired with teachers at her new high school for mentorship. The obvious assumption was that teachers at the low-performing schools were inadequate, inexperienced, or ill-prepared for the job.

My friend raised her hand and said, with what I'm sure was a somewhat sarcastic tone, "Does that mean I can mentor myself?" She referred, of course, to the fact that, although she had switched schools, her proficiency in teaching had not changed—only the *perception* of her proficiency against the backdrop of a different environment and student circumstances.

At the "higher-performing" school in which she had taught for 30 years, both she and her students won countless awards. But now, as a teacher at the less affluent school with more Title I students and services, was she suddenly somehow less proficient than before? (A more meaningful program might have been to swap the teachers entirely from one school to the other and compare relative improvement in test scores after a year.)

Teachers affect student achievement, but we are by no means the only—and probably not the most important—factor. For instance, if all other influences lean toward the opposite end of the spectrum—few families are at or below poverty level, the majority of children live in stable two-parent homes in neighborhoods with little or no crime, and few children come to school hungry, what would be the impact of a truly below-average teacher? Studies have shown that, on average, children, and therefore the school, perform well anyway.

A comprehensive multi-variate analysis would benefit virtually everyone. Data could be used at an individual student level to predict if he or she is at high risk for low achievement and to inform design of comprehensive individual plans. At a macro level, that data could assist in ongoing monitoring of the social changes occurring across a school, a district, or a state education system. Over time, that same data could provide substantiation for where more funding is needed and give local administrators more predictability with respect to everything from staffing needs to after-school programs, based on all of the factors in play.

Continuing research must be conducted to identify the societal factors impacting children, teachers, and schools across the country, in rural and urban areas, in areas of poverty and areas of affluence, in areas of high and low crime, and a meta-analysis performed. I would theorize that the same factors may have negligible effects in some locations while having major impacts in others, with moderate influences in still others, because I have seen the varying effects on individual students who have passed through my classroom these past two decades. In that same time frame, the school system has shifted from having a majority of white middle class students to a larger percentage of less financially stable minority students.

When considered as only one of multiple factors in an edu-system, the influence of the teacher on student learning would be measured on the basis of apple to apple comparisons. Expectations for job performance would then be based on realistic criteria against the background of the complex interactions at play in the school and classroom today.

For improvement to occur in "failing schools," honest and open conversations must take place, including whether or not the schools are, indeed failing—defined as not reaching an agreed-upon definition of success—and if so, why. We cannot look at teachers and poverty levels alone. We must consider all of the societal factors influencing the community, the students, and, by default, the school.

Dialogue must occur with no allowance for blame, and it must:

1. Identify factors, supported by research, that directly impact learning and the environment in which learning must occur;
2. Devise relevant benchmarks of progress and measurement schemes that are much more relevant than standardized tests, and
3. Remove responsibility and accountability from teacher proficiency evaluations for tasks they could not possibly do even if time were not an issue. Programs beyond the walls of the school must be undertaken and focused on addressing specific facets of the problems and collaboration invited.

Teachers are clearly key in the process, and must do their jobs, but accountability for performance must be aligned with only those things over which a teacher has control—what goes on in his or her classroom—and the rest of society—from parents to politicians—must be held accountable for their contributions to the problems we face.

The Spheres of Influence

There is a common agreement that the three legs of a child's education are the parents, teachers, and the student himself and that maximum potential for learning occurs when ALL are involved. There is no straight-line relationship; instead, there is a fluid, dynamic, and admittedly hard-to-define relationship among all the variables. Students are impacted/ influenced by parents and teachers and all are influenced by society.

The Venn diagram on the next page is a visualization of the interconnectedness of the most important people in a child's learning experience and the sphere of influence from societal factors.

Each societal influence within the sphere contributes to the learning potential of any given child in a school. However, some influences within the sphere are more powerful than others. If we assign degrees of influence within and between each of the influence scales, the "edu-system" becomes even more complex and dynamic.

- "Highest Learning" occurs where parents, students, and teachers converge and have positive influences on each other in spite of all the societal influences. The child is successful even if there are negative factors present because they have learned from parents and teachers how to overcome.
- "Lowest Learning" occurs when the influence of parent and teacher is low or non-existent, and the child is impacted by negative social factors.
- "Self Motivated Learners" are immune to the negative societal influences that impact other children. They will learn in spite of difficult home lives. The effectiveness of the teachers according to traditional measurements is almost irrelevant. These students will learn anyway.

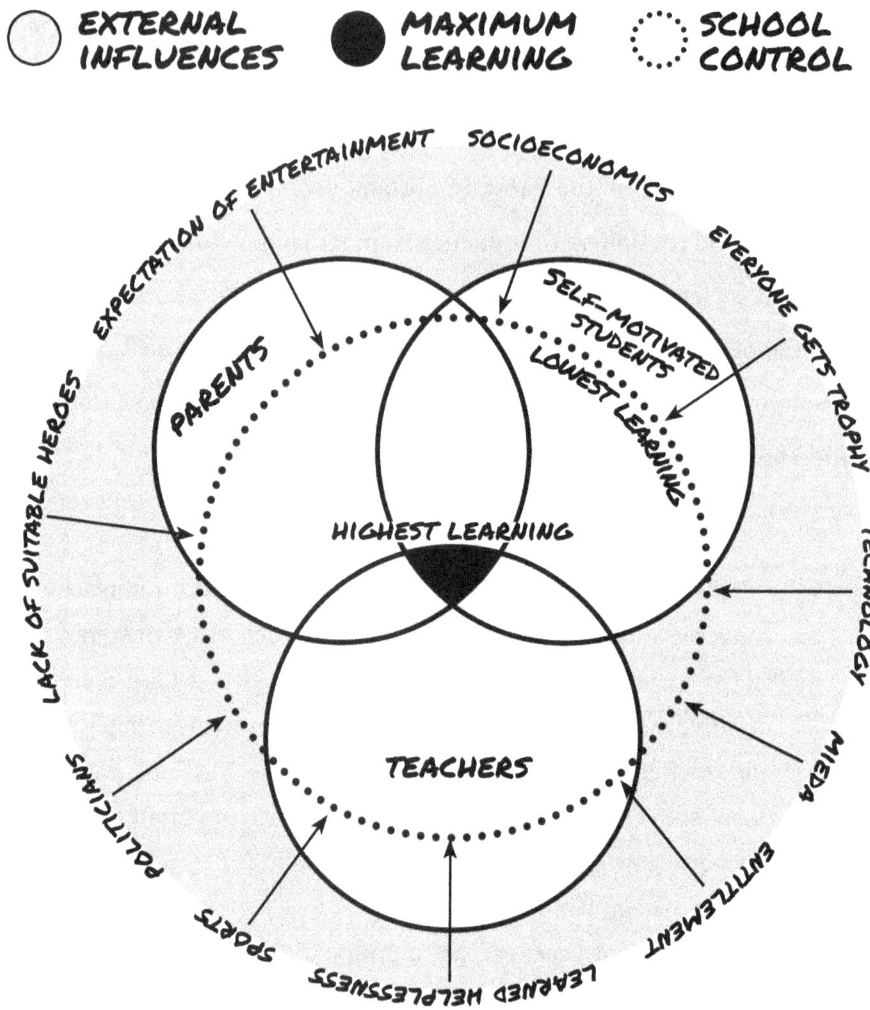

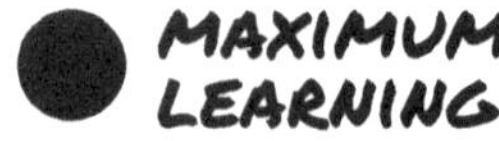

- "Self-Motivated Students" - Learners succeed regardless of external influences, including parent and/or teacher support
- "Lowest Learning Students" - Influenced by negative social and external circumstances with little or no mitigating influence from parents and teachers
- "Highest Learning Students" - Parents and teachers work together to achieve despite negative social and external circumstances

Although a mostly well-intended method for evaluating and funding schools, "No Child Left Behind" created a situation in which schools were classified as "failing" without any consideration of economic circumstances, crime rates, family stability, parental and community involvement, or any other local social influences we know have significant impacts on whether or not the basic and safety needs of the children in those schools. Scoring and ranking with test scores will always occur because people want a simple "score" to compare, and admittedly, some quantitative measurements should be a part of the picture. But far more needs to be considered when talking about public education. When schools are scored and ranked, the criteria used to rank schools should look more like the following instead of a single and limited measurement like standardized test scores alone.

Schools ranked in the future as "successful" or "high achieving" might also report that the majority of students come from:

- Families with both parents in a stable relationship
- Parents who are able to provide for basic needs of food, shelter, love and additional resources for extra-curricular activities
- Parents who graduated from post-secondary institutions
- Parents with jobs that pay far more than a livable wage

and that the schools exist in communities with:

- Active PTA/PTSA/PTO organizations and extracurricular "booster" clubs
- District and local administrators and school boards who communicate clear and realistic goals and are rated as supporting teachers to teach to their best methods

- A relatively low crime rate
- A majority of long-time residents and relatively few known transient families

Similarly, another school, designated as "failing" or "low achieving" might report that a high percentage of students come from:

- Households with one parent or other adult provider
- Parent(s) incapable of providing for basic needs of food, shelter, love
- Parent(s) who dropped out of high school
- Parent(s) employed in low-wage jobs

and that the school exists in communities with:

- Little or no involvement in educational support
- District and local administrators and school boards who regularly change goals, are inconsistent in communication, and mandate that teachers not vary outside the district or state curricula
- A relatively high rate of crime
- A substantial number of transient families

I know of cases where schools classified as not meeting the old "Annual Yearly Progress" goals where teachers were blamed for the school's "failure," and punitive measures resulted in every teacher being required to re-apply for his or her job, despite already exemplary careers. I have seen cases where districts and states "took over" schools and installed new leadership only to slide downward in rankings. The state government is threatening to take over several schools in Georgia as I write this.

The moral of this story is that we must begin to look at public education holistically, as an integrated system where each societal factor influences other societal factors, or the melees of the past decade and more will continue to negatively impact every teacher, every parent, every child.

Chapter 11
What's Next?

Above all, I hope I have struck a nerve or said something that helps motivate you, wherever you fit in this massive undertaking, to take action where you have authority and ability to do so.

Don't just stew over it, DO something about it. Public education needs everyone's involvement to get better. What is the purpose of public education? What do Americans want – high test scores or young adults with a good work ethic? Who should be the primary educators of our children—teachers, parents, the community? How should change occur? There are hundreds of issues and I truly believe hundreds of innovative solutions to be found, but unless we work together, things will just get worse, and the kids and our country will suffer.

Here's my first pass at a list of where we can begin.

Teachers: I have a job for you. Get active. Speak up. Get engaged. Quit sitting back and taking what everyone pushes our way as mandates, criticism, and abuse. Don't get nasty, defensive, aggressive, or obnoxious like so many do on the internet or "news" shows. Take the high road and engage critics in true dialogue, not arguments. The elected officials, parents, and communities need to hear our voices telling our stories, communicating our ideas and recommendations for the future of public education in America.

Register to vote and be at the polls every time there's a referendum or election. Slightly more than 50% of educators are registered and fewer than 30% make the effort and actually vote. There are millions of teachers in the United States. Add to that all the supporting staff in schools and the families of teachers, staff, administrators and that makes us the largest voting force in America. We don't have the money and lobbying strength that other professions have, but we have the numbers to make our voices be heard.

Otherwise, continue to settle for being on the receiving end of elected officials criticizing, cutting budgets, and blaming us for all that is going on in our places of work. Why do you think groups such as senior citizens, gun owners, and financial institutions get elected officials' attention and legislation more favorable to their agendas? *They lobby and vote en masse.*

Communicate. Talk our profession up every chance you get at ball games, parties, church, and over the back fence to neighbors. Write letters to parents, community leaders, and elected officials. Invite the media, business leaders, and parents into your classroom for a day to see what happens. Let them see everything that is involved in managing and teaching 30+ students at a time. Sign real petitions, mail real letters, and not just the ones on Facebook or Twitter. Make it personal and make it impossible to ignore. Visit the offices of administrators, school board members, superintendents, and elected officials and talk.

Elected officials: Talk to us. If you have a problem with how we are doing something, let us know and let us defend it. Quit using us to get votes. Quit decreasing funding levels and expecting more for less. Instead of improving the public education system in America, some of you have crippled us with your criticism, defunding, and micromanaging.

Parents: If you are happy with your schools and teachers—speak up. Tell everyone what you like and why. Tell local leaders what you want from your schools, academically and non-academically. If you are not happy, speak up and be specific. Don't generalize because that is what you heard from the media and at election time. We want to hear from you directly, not hear about ourselves in the news or at the ball park. Talk with us – don't yell and put us down behind our backs.

Community and business leaders: Speak up. What do you want from schools? Be detailed and be vocal. Don't sit back and complain that schools are failing you—be a part of the conversation to improve education. Do you want graduates who can do math and science or graduates who can read and write? Do you want schools to be community centers around which the families, businesses, and teachers coalesce to develop programs designed to actually teach children the knowledge and skills they will need to thrive in the world they will inherit? Or do you want lock-step mandated curricula aimed at high test scores that measure very little of relevance?

Researchers:

Most of the research in the news has been focused on how to improve school infrastructures, administrations, curricula, and teachers to increase "student success." I know there are researchers studying all of the factors we've discussed here and then some, but the information is not well-disseminated and application of findings not is not widespread. We need more studies whose focus is answering the following questions and media willing to cover the results more prominently.

- What are Americans' current definitions of student success? How do we define the purpose of public education so that it meets the needs and reasonable perceptions of ALL groups?
- What is the impact of negative external factors like poverty, lack of parental involvement and community crime on teacher effectiveness? How can we best minimize the impacts?
- What has been the impact of specific legislative directives that have been mandated over the last 30 years? Have they achieved their aims? If not, why not? If so, why? Have they helped all students or just single demographic groups? What have we learned?

- The trend is that teacher performance ratings increase/decrease after results of international/national tests are released. What impact does/has that public criticism by non-educators have on the development of new teachers and recruitment into the profession?
- What impacts do different parenting "types" have on child success? How can we promote healthy parent-teacher alliances?
- What has been the long-term impact, on the motivation of students and teachers, of the public belief that teachers are the primary problem with public education? If negative, how can we best work to change those beliefs?

There's no doubt that the answers are complex.

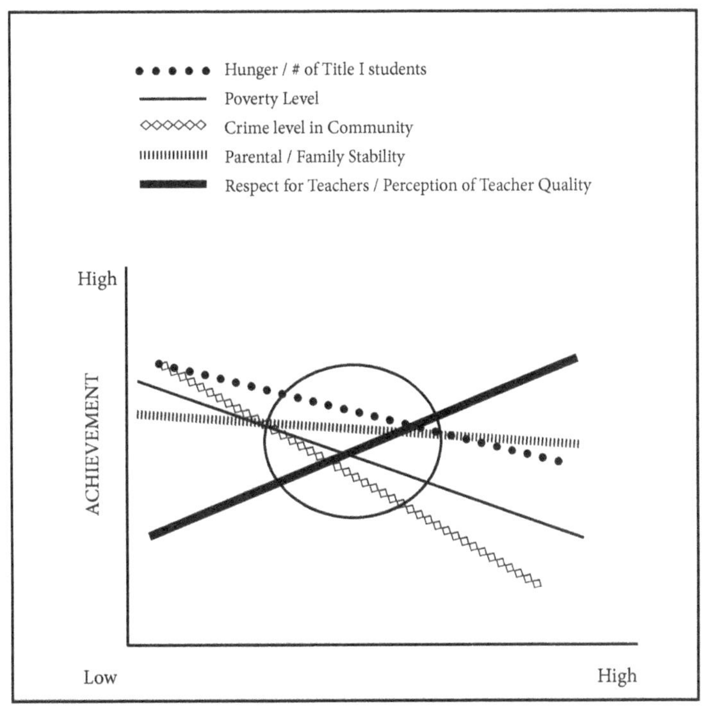

The Rest of Us: Every citizen of the United States needs to become a part of a constructive dialogue to bring about real improvement in public education. Blaming, false accusations, diminishing of those who are different, and micromanagement has obviously not worked and it will not work in the future.

An Army colonel once told me when I was working at Fort Benning, Georgia, "Mullen, if you are not a part of the solution, you are a part of the problem." Hence, the impetus for this book. Let's work together and restore public education to the place of respect it once held.

Chapter 12
Conclusion

Even today, in this highly politicized environment, if you ask most people who, outside of their parents, had the greatest positive impact in their lives, most will name a teacher.

The effect we can have, however, is increasingly limited in the face of the social and cultural changes occurring around us. However, we are not to blame for the negative influences on the children we teach. Every person called to be a teacher aspires to make a difference in all our students' lives, but we are dealing with real humans, not widgets that can be shaped and formed into value-added products in a manufacturing plant. Education doesn't happen in a vacuum and every "product" is a unique combination of aptitudes, skills, desires, and attitudes.

Before I launch into the meat of what I think lies ahead, let me start with the most important human lesson of all. We can't earn respect by demanding it. We must show it.

My fellow teachers, I thank you. Thank you for everything you do every day. I understand what you are experiencing to some degree. Thank you for talking to me in the hallways, at meetings, and one-on-one. I have been listening and trying to synthesize your stories for years, I hope I have done them justice here.

Thanks to my family and friends, too. You supported me when I came home exhausted and needed a nap before dinner; you gave me room to express my frustration and anger on days when the pressure was just too much; you understood when I missed a soccer game to grade papers or attend extra-curricular school activities in evenings, weekends, and summers.

To those friends still in the corporate world and strangers I met at meetings across the state, thank you for sharing your concerns. I have had many great conversations with you about public education, schools, and your children/grandchildren. You clearly want what is best for your family, community, and country. You admit that schools are not businesses and you are ready to help if needed in any way you can.

Elected officials: Thank you. I have talked with many of you. I believe that you want to help improve public education. I also understand that public education is but one of the often controversial topics you deal with when you are in session. You have helped me understand your world and the complexities of the position you hold. Please take some time to read this book to understand the complexities of our world.

To parents, thank you for trusting me to help your child grow and develop. You send me a 12-year-old and I return to you a teenager. It is a tough time for them and you. Through the years, I have talked with you in meetings, on the phone, and at ball fields. I have been listening. I know that most of you understand that public schools do the best they can with your child but at the same time have real concerns about the good and bad that happens.

No matter what situation you find yourself in, we know that we are the second most important influence in your children's lives, especially those in elementary school. We want to be partners with you in raising your children to reach their greatest potential.

Finally, to the most important people here—the children and youth I work with every day—thank you for being who you are. You are the reason I became a teacher and the reason, after 20 years, I'm still here. I know that you want to learn—I see it in your faces as you struggle with a problem, and I live for the smile and fist pump when you figure it out. I honor your courage when you come to school despite challenges I do not see.

You are growing up in a tough time in our world, one that is more complicated and challenging than the one that I grew up in, and one with opportunities I could not have imagined.

Even so, no matter what you may hear to the contrary from other students or adults, please know that your teachers truly want the absolute best for you.

What do we do now?

We were not the "nation at risk" suggested by President Reagan's report back in 1983, but I think we can safely say that the mission of public education, and the welfare of all of our citizens because of it, are at risk today. We Americans have not recognized that, along with our faith traditions, education is at the fulcrum of our society, and have not protected it from the political football it has become. Instead, we have wasted precious time and energy, and have brought ourselves closer to the edge of an abyss that was only in the imagination of politicians three decades ago.

Instead of considering the results of that 1983 study as what they were—a statistical snapshot of where U.S. students as a whole and as members of different demographic groups and the rest of the world—we seem to have launched into a generation of blaming everyone, especially teachers, for the income-achievement gap, racial gaps, gender gaps, you name it. This has resulted in policies that assume that the education of our children can be reduced to a process on an assembly line.

In the meantime, by government-driven "reform" initiatives like "No Child Left Behind," "Race to the Top," and other well-intentioned but ill-advised misapplications of business principles where they have no business being applied, we have watched as the income gaps have widened, and our ranking on international tests go down instead of up. We have thrown money at technology as our savior, with the expectation that computers and tablets can substitute for human contact. And we have turned to numbers derived from pencil marks on machine-scored tests as a primary measurement of mastery.

Conclusion

While we spent time teaching students to take tests, we created still other gaps, like the one between high school seniors and college freshmen regarding the complexity of written material they must be able to digest. Many seniors, accustomed to memorizing small bits of information to pass tests and graduate, are ill-prepared for college. The push to raise test scores and graduate 100% has resulted in most high school students not having to read, write, or think on an advanced level in order to earn a diploma.

Accepting the fact that every student is wonderfully different from every other, school improvement programs and initiatives must be student centered. We must put egos aside and develop solid plans through honest communication and consensus. We must silence the critics and cynics that have access to microphones because their self-righteous agendas and boisterous negativity is toxic.

Reform will not be an easy job, nor will it be painless. It will require that we look in the mirror and do some soul-searching about what service we truly want public education to perform and the outcomes we desire and then honestly assess whether what we believe we want is possible or productive.

It will not be completed during this election cycle or the next or the next after that, as new standards and obstacles and opportunities will continue to present themselves. But it must be approached with the awareness that education is (and always has been) an edu-system affecting every part of our society. All who are affected—namely every citizen—*must* take ownership of the parts we play, be given authority to change the things we as experts over those areas know must be changed, and be held accountable for the results, good or bad, of those solutions.

When we make mistakes, and we most assuredly will, we must learn from our mistakes and adjust the course, just as we would if while on a trip we discover we've gone down the wrong road. We must retrace our steps, find a new way to achieve the goals we set, and move forward.

As teachers, we accept the responsibility of creating a classroom environment in which learning can ideally take place. As teachers, we accept the responsibility of staying abreast of advances in our chosen fields and knowledgeable about the art and science of learning and educational pedagogy. As teachers, we accept the responsibility as the "second-most" influential people in the lives of the children we teach.

But we cannot ensure that our students are fed when they are not with us. We cannot ensure that our students are safe in the hours they are not with us. We cannot ensure that our students get enough sleep at night, assuming they have a bed in which to sleep in the first place. We can't help students instantly overcome ADHD and learning disabilities, close gaps in reading or math in a single year, or magically get ESL students up to speed so they score comparably to English-speaking students on standardized tests validated in English.

But we *can*:

1. **Risk trusting each other again and refusing to let naysayers poison the process;**
2. **Re-examine and agree on a purpose of public education that considers all of our needs and all of our definitions of success;**

3. Inventory the current state of affairs with respect to the delivery of the outcomes defined in #2 and review research about how we may get from where we are to there (and how we won't)—irrespective of which groups or what policies politicians and shock-jocks insist are to blame;
4. Engage in dialogue and debate about policy initiatives—what educators can realistically be expected to achieve based on what we already know—with careful attention to what negative unintended consequences may result and plans to offset those consequences and adjust our course as needed;
5. Ensure that the dialogue is between people with demonstrated expertise in every area of life that touches teachers and students, from poverty and abuse to the future knowledge and skills required in the workplace, but excluding politicians whose only focus is reelection, media outlets that have lost journalistic integrity, and anyone else with the clear objective of dividing us into pockets of "we" vs. "them";
6. Return to a shared common sense with respect to the value of achievement, encourage motivation toward mastery, and reward effort;
7. Restore the respect for education and educators deserve for the roles we serve in touching the life of every school-aged child in our country—whether he's in a public or private school, lives in an urban or rural area, is poor, middle class, or affluent, is college-bound, tech-school bound, or workplace bound, and above all…

8. **Stop blaming others, take responsibility for what we can influence, and start talking.**

In the appendix, I list a series of questions under each category to "prime the pump" for us to think about the topics and issues that face us and begin the difficult but necessary dialogue required to develop a comprehensive plan for positively impacting all of the issues that stand in the way of improving public education. The stakes are indeed high, but there are no quick fixes and the measurement of success of public education initiatives cannot be reduced to scores on a test. If we do that hard work, the test scores and rankings will take care of themselves.

Going forward, we must honestly examine everything we do, every policy we make for its ramifications on all factors impacting the education of our children. We know, and have known, for some time, what effects the social, emotional, cultural, and neurological issues have on children's ability to acquire the skills and knowledge they need—it's time we worked together to address them. And it's time we did it together.

Teachers can only do so much. We've been bashed for too long, bearing the brunt of far more than we can realistically be held accountable for. But we're still here, we're still committed to helping prepare the children of our country to not only survive, but thrive in the world they will inherit.

Let's get started!

Appendix
Questions to Get Us Started

For each action item mentioned in the Conclusion, I have listed below sample questions I think we need to ask ourselves and all stakeholders who will be involved in the dialogue. These will naturally spawn more questions that are crucial to the dialogue. This is just a beginning.

Visit my website **www.TeacherTimMullen.com** for more information about how, in the next few weeks and months, we can start the dialogue.

1. **Risk trusting each other again and refusing to let naysayers poison the process.**

    a. What/who do you think caused the trust to be broken which has resulted in education not being as effective as it could have been without those negative influencers?

    b. Who do you trust to be a part of this dialogue to improve education in America? Who don't you trust?

    c. Is there anything we can do to regain those who don't trust teachers? Be detailed.

    d. What would those we don't trust have to do to regain our trust? Be detailed.

    e. Based on who you think will try to poison the dialogue, what can be done to minimize/neutralize their toxicity?

    f. Are there organizations, groups, and/or individuals you do not trust to be a part of the dialogue to improve education in America? Why?

2. **Re-examine and agree on the purpose of public education that considers all of our needs and all of our definitions of success.**

    a. What do you think is the purpose of public education in America?
    b. What are some goals we should think about for public education that include the purpose(s) you stated in 'a' above?
    c. In a sentence, define success.
    d. What goals/outcomes do you believe are attainable? Which ones do you believe aren't attainable? Why and why not?

3. **Inventory the current state of affairs with respect to the delivery of the outcomes defined in #2 and review research about how we may get from where we are to there (and how we won't) – irrespective of which groups or what policies politicians and shock-jocks insist are to blame.**

    a. **What research do you know about that contributes to defining success and/or establishing goals for the purpose and success of public education in America?**
    b. **Detail/reference any efforts you know of that have attempted to define the purpose of education and/or success so we can examine their efforts and build upon.**

4. **Engage in dialogue and debate about policy initiatives—what educators can realistically expect to achieve based on what we already know—with careful attention to what negative unintended consequences may result and plans to offset those consequences and adjust our course as needed.**

    a. What policy initiatives do you think should be discussed first?
    b. What initiatives should be held until later? Do you think later because they are not as important the others or you think the reaction would be so negative they would derail other conversations? Explain.
    c. Where should these dialogues begin? Be detailed.
    d. Who should be included/not included and why/why not?
    e. What other ideas do you have that might be used to prevent dialogue from becoming derailed and/or for redirecting toxicity if it enters the dialogue?

5. **Ensure that the dialogue is between people with demonstrated expertise in every area of life that touches teachers and students, from poverty and abuse to the future knowledge and skills required in the workplace, but excluding politicians whose focus is reelection, media outlets that have lost journalistic integrity; and anyone else with the clear objective of dividing us into pockets of "we' vs. "them."**

    a. Who do you think needs to be a part of the dialogue (be specific)?
    b. Who should moderate the dialogue? Why them?
    c. Are there some politicians that need to be a part of the dialogue? Who? Why them and not others?
    d. Is there a role for media? What should there role entail? Are there certain media outlets that should, and not, be included? Why?
    e. Who else should be included in the dialogue? Why? Who should not be included in the dialogue? Why not?

6. **Return to a shared common sense with respect to the value of achievement, encourage motivation toward mastery, and reward effort.**

   a. **What are your thoughts of giving awards to students for participation versus reserving awards for those that excel, and/or win the competition?**
   b. **How does a teacher determine if a child achieves mastery (for skills, knowledge, or other mastery goal?). What does it 'look like?'**

7. Restore the respect for education and that educators deserve for the roles we serve in touching the life of every school-aged child in our country—whether he's in a public or private school, lives in an urban or rural area, is poor, middle class, or affluent, is college-bound, tech-school bound, or workplace bound.

   a. What type of respect is more important for us (teachers)? There is the type of respect expected to be given to people because of their positions/roles (teachers, police, doctors, etc.) and respect that is earned through one demonstrating their skills, compassion, and honor over time.
   b. What do you think has led to the decline of either form of respect for teachers?
   c. What do we (teachers) need to do to regain the respect of the public?

8. **Stop blaming others, take responsibility for what we can influence, open our ears to each other, accept constructive criticism, and start talking.**

    a. Are there some people that you think will never stop blaming teachers? Who and why do you think this?
    b. What can we do with those that will always blame? (We cannot change people so need to have a plan to continue in spite of them).
    c. Are there some people that you think will never take responsibility with whatever their role is with regard to education? Who and why do you think this?
    d. What can we do with those that will never take responsibility, with whatever their roles is with regard to education? (We cannot change people so need to have a plan to continue in spite of them).

About the Author
Tim Mullen

I have been married for 32 years to Loretta Mirandola. A lawyer for 18 years, she followed me into education and retired at the end of the 2015-2016 school year. We have three daughters: Martina, Jacqueline, and Alexandra. Martina and Jacqueline are married and live in New York. Alexandra lives in Atlanta. Loretta and I live in Lawrenceville, Georgia.

I am a public school teacher. I teach Life Science to seventh graders. As I indicated in the text of the book, I have not always been a teacher. I did not actually have an education degree until my 14th year of teaching, when I received my Ph.D. I was in my late 30s when I began certification coursework for the transition to the classroom.

I had two prior careers before teaching: 1) as a federal civil servant with the Department of Defense (Army for 7 years), and 2) in computer software sales and management for a rapidly growing company (7 years). I have a B.S. in Environmental Resources Management, an M.S. in Public Administration, and a Ph.D. in Middle School Education.

But now, front and center, I am a teacher. I am not, however, a teacher who:

- is disgruntled,
- is unhappy,
- is wanting to lash out,
- is angry,
- is unhappy with my leaders (my superintendent, Board of Education, Principal),
- wants to stir things up, or
- writing this book out of anger, revenge, or dissatisfaction with my working conditions.

But I *am* concerned for the future of public education in America. There are all sorts of so-called "experts" who say they know what is wrong and how public education should be fixed, but the voice I do not hear is of the only true experts on education—teachers.

I have been involved with Georgia's largest teacher organization as a board member and as president, so I have attended meetings throughout Georgia and listened to teachers tell their stories. I have had access to school superintendents, school board members, legislators, business leaders, and various education organizations from throughout the state and discussed many of the topics covered within this book. My National Board Certification trained me to be tuned in with my students, their parents, and the professional community.

I am writing from a good place in my life. I like my job, what I teach, and the people I work with daily. I could not ask for a better assistant principal, building principal, district superintendent, or Board of Education. I feel trusted by my leaders and am asked regularly for my input at all levels by district leaders. I now have more than 20 years in the classroom and look back with no regrets for switching into the teaching profession.

In fact, my primary passion in life these days is working with students. I like them, their parents, and my fellow teachers. There are naturally a few students and parents who require more attention than others and I welcome the questions and concerns of parents who want to be involved in their children's education. If you are a teacher and your experience has been different from mine, if you've seen or experienced things that underscore what I've said here or challenge my perspective, please communicate them with me—I want to hear. Please join the conversation.

Contact me by visiting the website at:

www.TeacherTimMullen.com

To order additional copies of

STOP BLAMING + START TALKING

please

visit the website at

www.TeacherTimMullen.com

or

www.Amazon.com

Volume discounts are available through the author.

Email us at

Quantities@TeacherTimMullen.com